My Life in Prison

An Education of the Heart

Toni Ukkerd Carter

BALBOA
PRESS
A DIVISION OF HAY HOUSE

Balboa Press books may be ordered through booksellers or by contacting:

Balboa Press
A Division of Hay House
1663 Liberty Drive
Bloomington, IN 47403
www.balboapress.com
1 (877) 407-4847

Because of the dynamic nature of the Internet, any web addresses or links contained in this book may have changed since publication and may no longer be valid. The views expressed in this work are solely those of the author and do not necessarily reflect the views of the publisher, and the publisher hereby disclaims any responsibility for them.

The author of this book does not dispense medical advice or prescribe the use of any technique as a form of treatment for physical, emotional, or medical problems without the advice of a physician, either directly or indirectly. The intent of the author is only to offer information of a general nature to help you in your quest for emotional and spiritual well-being. In the event you use any of the information in this book for yourself, which is your constitutional right, the author and the publisher assume no responsibility for your actions.

Any people depicted in stock imagery provided by Thinkstock are models, and such images are being used for illustrative purposes only. Certain stock imagery © Thinkstock.

Print information available on the last page.

ISBN: 978-1-5043-4312-1 (sc)
ISBN: 978-1-5043-4313-8 (e)

Balboa Press rev. date: 11/25/2015

A Correctional Teacher's
True Stories
Folsom State Prison, California

Toni Ukkerd Carter

Educating the mind without educating the heart
is no education at all. −*Aristotle*

Acknowledgements

This book was a production brought to you by all who helped me through the writing process with their particular gifts and encouragements no matter how big or how small.

Cover and inside photographs compliments of the California Department of Corrections and Rehabilitation

Dedication

This book is dedicated to my son,
Coye E. Carter, for his unconditional
Love and support;
And to souls everywhere who
Long to be free!

Contents

Folsom Sign at the Prison Road Entrance

CHAPTER 1

Introduction

All of our humanity is dependent upon recognizing the humanity in others. Archbishop Desmond Tutu

There are many kinds of life sentences in the State of California. During the two decades I spent teaching in prison, I met individuals with just about every type of life sentence that a person can receive. It did not take long to realize that those who work in prisons are doing a type of life sentence also. It may not have been a sentence of 20 years to life, but it was a life sentence. Of course there are major differences. Without realizing it, I was taking the prison home until someone at home reminded me, "We are not incarcerated!" I learned to conscientiously check that mentality at the prison gate as I left each day and not bring that drama home. The thoughts we entertain on a daily basis can create personal prisons long before bars and walls ever do. It's important to be aware of our thoughts all the time.

Curiosity over education in prison and prison itself continues to be of interest to many people I encounter everywhere. Over time, friends, acquaintances, and strangers would ask about my workdays and seemed to enjoy the stories I shared from behind the granite walls of this State Correctional Facility. Over time, many have asked about my days and after hearing a story or two, the encouragement to write about my experiences became a compelling goal. People were always curious about things that had become second nature to me, and they were full of questions as well as worries. This book is an attempt to answer some of those questions and ally some of those fears.

Typically, the first question most people asked was, "Do you teach incarcerated men or women?" Of course, Folsom State Prison located not far from California's capital, Sacramento, is an all male prison at both the "New Folsom" and "Old Folsom" facilities. Both sites used to fall under the umbrella of one prison. However, circa 1992, changes began to happen in a big way. One of the changes was to divide the New from the Old so that there were now two prisons with two wardens, and two of everything else. This was an interesting process and one that affected the Education Program as it was also divided. Another change that happened circa 2011 was that a small group of female prisoners were moved onto the grounds at a minimum facility. This facility is somewhat isolated from the main sections of both prisons.

As a teacher for the State, I was far removed from any decision making process. I barely got to decide what I taught on a daily basis. I know the decision to locate female prisoners on the grounds probably had to do with space, or the lack of space throughout the correctional system.

Someone once asked if I taught the children of the guards? No, the correctional officers' children are not in prison, nor do they live at the prison. There is a small complement of houses on grounds to accommodate special personnel staffing needs.

The next two-fold question was always, "Who are "they", and what are "they" like?" My response was always: "They" are your fathers and husbands, your brothers and uncles, and your sons and nephews." Without hesitation, everyone would shake their heads in agreement and understanding. Personally, seeing me separated from the rest of humankind is not a healthy indulgence. Different, Yes! But, we are all members of the human race. These days, just about everyone in California knows of some human being who is in prison, has been to prison, or maybe on the way to prison based on their choices.

At the time of writing this Edition, some of the laws which fostered mass incarceration have eased a bit, such as "Three Strikes." And, the Federal mandate that required the State of California, Department of Corrections and Rehabilitation (CDC&R) to release tens of thousands of prisoners was upheld. Therefore, prisons are slowly and quietly returning to reasonable levels.

However, there will always be stories to write. The new stories have been included with some of the First Edition stories that I took the liberty of expanding and or adding follow ups to particular stories. I trust you will enjoy the old ones with new eyes.

These stories are not a Hollywood creation; they are stories straight outta Folsom State Prison. This book provides a brief description of some of the experiences I have had over the years. Each anecdotal story is true from my perspective and my experience. I hope they serve to provide a bit of insight into the lives of incarcerated men who are either permanently or temporarily barred from enjoying life in society. Perhaps you will also find a bit of inspiration for your own life and a reminder that freedom that you enjoy should be appreciated every day.

While the First Edition contained a plethora of quotes that I used in the classroom to motivate and inspire my students, the Second Edition gets right to the stories with only a few quotes sprinkled in to enhance a point. I used quotes daily in the classroom because they had the potential to provoke new ways of thinking or to interrupt old cognitive patterns if only for a moment. Students were always encouraged to leave a corner of their minds open to new information. I looked for these openings to inject words of wisdom. In other words, the quotes were used as educational appetizers to whet the intellect. I then set my intention to work on their hearts.

In all cases, **the names in the stories have been changed for the comfort and protection of everyone. The two exceptions are in: Chapter 7-- The Stroke and Chapter 24—Saved The Best For Last.** The stories are offered to provide a bit of insight into the lives of incarcerated men who are either permanently or temporarily barred from enjoying life in society. It is my hope that you will find these personal experiences satisfying to your curiosity, tickling to your funny bone, liberating to your thoughts, and inspiring to your life. Like most experiences, they are snapshots in words.

CHAPTER 2

Harmony Grits

It is not enough to have a good mind, the main
thing is to use it well. —Rene Descartes

Good teachers have to learn how to be good motivators. It's that simple and yet that complex. Many incarcerated adults did not want to be in educational programs for a variety of reasons. They could be on a work detail that paid twelve or fifteen cents an hour; they could be sleeping the days away in their cells; or they could be hanging out on the yard with their buddies. However, if there was no evidence in their file of a high school diploma, school was the recommended program. My adult learners loved to ask, "What good is this going to do me?" It did not matter what the subject was, the question was the same.

Working under a system of open enrollment meant students could be assigned to my class at any given time. Therefore, I needed to be ready for men of all ages, all nationalities and religions, all educational and socio-economic backgrounds, all sorts of gang affiliations, and those who have engaged in all types of felonious behaviors that were far more salacious and despicable than I cared to write about. A teacher had to bring about some sense of harmony and create an atmosphere for learning.

The one thing that piqued my awareness about many of the incarcerated men I worked with was that after months, and perhaps even years of always being told what to do and where to be, they continued to look for direction at every turn. This especially applied to men who had not completed their education. I figured that many of my students have been looking for the right direction all their life and got lost along the way. Now they were in prison and still looking to be directed. They seemed to be seeking something they were not even aware of themselves. They wanted someone they could trust to point the way.

During my teacher training days at Wayne State University in Michigan, it was my intention to teach business related subjects in a high school and eventually wind up in a college or university. I began on that track in Detroit. When I relocated to Sacramento, no one could have convinced me that my teaching career would take a left turn to prison education. Like most people, I was not even aware of the adult education programs in the California Correctional System.

Once I was working in the system, I slowly began to understand the degree of illiteracy. In many instances, I had students who already had high school diplomas, GEDs and in a couple of instances that I am aware of, Bachelor's degrees. Yet, they still couldn't read and comprehend at the 12th grade level. I began working at the prison in 1989, and I just knew I would eventually work myself out of the job. Little did I realize, the numbers of functionally illiterate would continue to climb—there was always a waiting list for school. I definitely had my work cut out for me, and this work, teaching in prison, allowed me to grow spiritual wings.

Little did I know I would still be teaching in prison twenty years later. In the beginning, I felt that if I could walk this journey for five years, it would be more than I could bear. After five years, I could say that I had given the adventure the good old college try. I would have been ready to move onward and upward. However, somewhere around year ten, I discovered that my thinking had changed. I realized the Universe had me right where I was supposed to be to fulfill my life's purpose which was to be a light in this particular area of darkness. I was then that I felt in alignment with that purpose. The realization came as a relief as I no longer had to find ways to escape from prison. Rather, I could look for ways to exemplify the true spirit of teaching and to keep finding ways to enjoy and motivate students.

Teachers in prison must learn to develop skills that conform to institutional regulations and still allow for learning to occur. They have to adhere to a fine line of motivating and inspiring students without becoming overly familiar. Anyone who has ever served time in prison knows the experience of being incarcerated is not pleasant on any level. I have seen some of the bravest and boldest crumble into emotional pieces. These are the emotional pieces the teachers have to work with as they strive to teach. It does not matter if the sentence was one year or a lifetime, the men are changed beings. An outside family member or friend will never know what their loved one has suffered because they have not walked a mile in those prison boots and shower shoes.

These human beings who may have committed some of the most heinous crimes imaginable were my students. They may have been on drugs or alcohol they may have come from a stable family background, and they may have been dropouts. In spite of any of these factors, I had to blend compassion with academics. Compassion does not equal stupidity or a false sense of security. It did mean being an empathetic presence who could work to reflect back to the individual the essence of who they are. So, somewhere between the massive amounts of paperwork that only a government bureaucracy can generate, and the incarcerated students who would rather spend the day doing something else, teaching had to occur.

There is a BIBLE passage that rang loudest during my time in prison and stayed in my mind: "...just as you did it to one of the least of these who are members of my family, you did it to Me." (Matthew 25:40, NRSV). I also realized that if it were my child, I would want a kind, compassionate person to be there along the path to provide positive input. One never knows when compassion can serve as a pivotal point to move life forward for good. There is no giving without receiving. And, like it or not, this is how our Universe operates.

For me, this is not an account from the naïve. I discovered early on that the face prisoners present to me as a non-custody staff can sometimes be very different than what they showed the establishment or each other. How I read or write about these behaviors is one thing. How the Universe reads and responds is something else. What I would like people to remember is that nothing escapes the vibrations of the

Universe. Try as we may, absolutely no one escapes. Our magnificent Universe is always listening to our thoughts and responding to us accordingly.

Living In Prison

The day in and day out grind of prison is not for the faint of heart. During the late 1990s, I had a clerk—all teacher clerks are prisoners—who seemed as gentle as a lamb. He was in his early 50s, kind, patient, considerate, and helpful at all times. He was told by a certain segment of the prisoner population that prison would toughen him up, and he would not leave the same person. By the time he paroled, he had become wiser but not tougher. He would remind me that he was actually trying his best to have fun in prison. It reminded him of his days in the Navy—always dressed in blue jeans and blue shirts, always being told what to do, where to be, and what to eat. Obviously, this is not the typical prison experience.

Once a prisoner awakes to the trauma of prison life, they are left to explore survival tactics as best as they can. I used the term "Awakes" because it seems that many prisoners enter the prison gates still stunned over being there and dazed over the amount of time they have to serve. This stunned state is what I call a penal coma. The person goes through daily motions without emotion, because emotions could be mistaken for weakness.

A normal day may begin at 5 a.m. to the sound of an ear piercing bell, followed by a loud voice over the PA system. This is the wakeup call for breakfast. Within 10 to 15 minutes an officer will unlock cell doors so prisoners can proceed to the dining hall. Because Folsom is the second oldest prison in California (since 1880), there are no modern, electronically controlled systems. Trying to retrofit the institution would be tantamount to building a new facility.

After sitting with a tray of morning mystery delicacies, an officer is right there to hurry everyone along to their work program or a return to their cells, if it's too early for work or school. For the masses that do not have a work program, their time is spent back in their small cells or on the yard. Each person picks up a "sack lunch" from a crate as they exit the dining hall to eat at noontime.

Students attending school must report at 7 a.m. (schedules can and have changed throughout the years). The usual school day is 6.5 hours and the student to teacher ratio is 27 to 1 in both Academic and Vocational programs. This routine varied to increase teacher loads: see Chapter 10. Each of the 33 State Prisons has an education program that is different in number of teachers and types and number of programs. Once the school or work day is over, prisoners return to their cells and afternoon showers begin.

At some point during the late afternoon comes the time many prisoners love, yet many others hate—mail call. For those who still have the love and support from family and friends, coveted news from home is passed out and read as part of their daily or weekly salvation. For those who have nothing coming from home or anywhere else, it's a time to find out from other men in an attempt to live vicariously through the news of others.

Next, a head count is initiated by three sounds of the institutional whistle which sounds like a train whistle. This lets all five housing units know that the mandatory institutional standing count is to begin. Officers must go cell to cell to see the inmate physically standing in his cell. Once everyone has been counted, each unit calls a central location to confirm. At that time, an actual old fashioned bell is rung 13 times to signal that no one has made the daring attempt to scale the fortified granite walls or razor wired fences to escape. Then, all housing units begin preparing to release prisoners for the evening meal.

After dinner, higher custody prisoners are returned to their cells. For them, the only out-of-cell experience for the rest of the evening is for phone calls if it is their turn in the unit's rotation. The larger numbers of medium custody prisoners can take advantage of the exercise yard or evening programs. These programs consist of AA, NA, religious services, and a few victim/offender type classes. Without positive programming, the dark side of prison culture takes over and a life of turmoil tends to persist. A person has to want to take advantage of the available programs for self-improvement and rehabilitation in order for the program to be of benefit.

The above description is a normal day. At any moment, a normal day can turn into a complete fiasco because someone woke up on the wrong side of their bunk. Depending on the severity of the disturbance, meaning racial fights, food fights, insanity fights, and so forth, the institution can quickly go into lockdown mode where prisoner movement comes to a halt. During serious lockdowns, prison staff is ready to assume other duties as assigned. The length of a lockdown depends on the magnitude of the disturbance, the individuals involved, and results of the investigation.

During high security times, lockdowns were a common occurrence. Some were so lengthy I forgot who my students were. By the time class returned, many had been unassigned with new faces in their place. It was always my feeling that a day with my class was far better than any day on lockdown. In the early part of the century, teachers were expected to walk the tiers during lockdowns to pass out homework and or provide instruction at the cell doors. The housing units were hot, smelly, and loud with constant activity. Medical visits, showers, meal distributions to name a few things made housing units like bee hives. Therefore, teachers in front of cell doors trying to provide instruction did not go over big. Every day in prison offered something different. I never knew what surprises awaited when I walked through the front gate. I always prayed for the best but was prepared to roll with the worst. It is a blessing to share some of those happy and interesting experiences with you in this book.

Heart Lesson ~ My thinking makes me captain of my ship. I am steadfast in keeping my thoughts positive and productive. I teach best when I walk my talk.

Main Academic Education Building—
My work world at prison.

CHAPTER 3

How Do You Spell Fun?

*The body heals with play, the mind heals with laughter
and the Spirit heals with joy" – Proverb*

Before going to work in prison, I knew and had faith in my Spiritual understanding. I understood that the only real power was in that Infinite Source from which all things flow, including us. God has been known by many names and the name you choose to call the Supreme Alpha and Omega is not nearly as important as understanding It, as well as understanding you are a direct descendent of It. If there is a religion that helps you with this understanding that you enjoy, that's fine. There are many paths to understanding. Our responsibility as humans is to not get lost on the path.

I knew that prison was full of many who were lost on the path. I knew that I would be connecting with them on the level of teacher/student. I wanted this to be my opportunity to do what I was born to do—teach! If I was being directed to prison, then that's where this Universe felt that I could be the most effective. This was going to be my connecting point to remind my students of who they really were and of their God given gifts to navigate life. I always tried to teach that whatever it is you are doing, do it to the best of your God-given ability. If it's for good and you are doing your best and enjoying the work, all good things in life will find you including money!

All students living in this particular gated community known as Folsom State Prison, could sense early on who worked at the prison for the paycheck and who worked because they enjoyed the work. I felt that I was scrutinized every minute of every work day by students, as well as staff, supervisors, and administrators. My movements about the prison were duly noted on a regular basis. The students knew they had time to put me through a series of tests to see where I stood on teaching, how I felt about prisoners and the prison itself, and my stance on all sorts of social issues.

The custody staff was checking to be sure my attire was appropriate. I could not wear anything resembling "inmate" clothing. They were also checking to see if I was where I was supposed to be during work hours. If I headed out of the gate before time was up, someone somewhere was on the phone reporting it. Of course there were a variety of reasons why it may have been necessary to leave early that had to be approved by the supervisors. The prison relished spies, snitches, rats, or whatever name you have for those reporting on others.

There was a time I and a fellow teacher walked over to the new prison which happened to be a 5-7 minute walk through a staff residential area. Before we got back, the education supervisors knew we had made the walk. We only went to get a cup of coffee during prep time. We were told we could not leave the education building during prep time any more. Never mind the fact that there was no space for teachers to do prep work. My colleague and I wound up pulling student desks into the women's room and trying to work there—grading papers and preparing class assignments for the week.

The teaching staff was always observing that I was not sitting, standing, moving too close to students and showing everyone fair and equal treatment. In an all male prison, the female staff was given extra scrutiny. There was one female teacher who was having a talk with her clerk. Someone reported that they were the only ones in the classroom and she appeared to be sitting too close to him. After that little fiasco, we had a male teacher facetiously walk around with a yardstick to be sure no one got too close to anyone else.

Supervisors checked to be sure I was reporting to work, teaching, keeping track of all records, and promoting and testing on a regular basis. At the time, education was a system that punished all teachers for the act(s) of one. Rewards and accolades were few and far in between. So, if someone showed up late to work repeatedly, all teachers had to do a double sign in—one at the entrance gate and one in education—all the time. If one teacher was caught showing non-educational videos, all teachers hence forth had to develop detailed lesson plans for approval before showing a video regardless of the video. The torment never stopped because there was always a rebel who pushed the envelope.

I was sent home once because the coat I was wearing was wearing a full-length, periwinkle which one officer determined was too close in color to prisoner chambray shirts. That meant I either had to put the coat in my car and go without a coat for the day, or go home to change coats. I was particularly surprised because I had been wearing the coat every winter for a few years and had never been stopped any other time. On this particular day, I decided that it was too cold to be without a coat, and if I went home, I was staying. Therefore, I opted for a relaxing day at home, and I returned the next day refreshed in a brown coat.

Prison administrators were checking that I did not bring any type of contraband onto prison grounds. After a number of people were caught bringing in drugs, tobacco, cell phones, and only heaven knows what else, the prison decided they had better start checking employee carry in bags. Just about everyone carried a bag of some type as there were no food services for employees. We had to bring our food and anything else we may need for the day. Some days I needed a sweater, or a jug of water, or school supplies such as construction paper, stencils, poster board for class projects.

On one surprise, I mean unannounced search, I had my newspaper confiscated as "contraband." That meant that the rules changed and no one told me. As a teacher, I used the newspaper for wonderful articles that served as essay topics, or sales ads that provided real life math problems and a wealth of other activities to keep the "adult learner" engaged. Never mind the fact that there were many prisoners who had newspaper/magazine subscriptions, and the library had newspapers from a variety of places delivered every day.

As disturbing as this policy was to me, I had to also remember that these clever minds also knew how to fashion weapons from newspapers so I couldn't be too upset. The on grounds prison museum is full of confiscated weapons made from the most innocuous items. The upsetting part was that everyone wanted to do your thinking for you! I didn't have enough sense to be sure I brought the paper back out with me. Well, I did, but there were others who did not have the sense or the desire.

On this day, all confiscated items were sealed in a manila envelope with your name on it and taken to the warden's office. That's where you had to go to retrieve your contraband after work. I heard that several of those envelopes were ringing all day long from the personal cell phones which were also considered contraband. I was glad I did not have to explain anything but a newspaper. My day had not even begun, and I was already having more fun than ever.

Heart Lesson ~ In life the man made laws and rules change frequently. Universal Law never changes. I love knowing that I can be flexible in life so that life will not break me.

Officer's Station inside the education building. In general, a school atmosphere is maintained during the day. Officer is responsible for the overall safty and security of staff and students in the building at all times.

CHAPTER 4

Happy Against The Odds

Thousands of candles can be lighted from a single candle,
and the life of the candle will not be shortened. Happiness
never decreases by being shared. —Buddha

I never met a person who was happy to be doing time in prison. Yet, somewhere along the line, many learned to be happy in spite of their circumstances. Not only is it a challenge to be unhappy every day, it is against our basic nature. Being in prison for one year or for life was enough of a situation to come to grips with, but having any kind of physical disability seemed to compound matters. From where I sat, many of the difficulties were because of the antiquated prison policies and the antiquated physical structure of "Old" Folsom Prison.

Yet, I met many men doing their best to endure their predicament while serving time. Since I could not imagine how these men coped, I did not even try. I worked to stay focused on creating positive experiences in the learning environment, because that's what I was paid to do. And, happy was how I chose to it.

I once met a prisoner without a foot! In place of his foot was a wooden stump that protruded from the bottom of his leg at ankle level. He walked with a cane. He would often say, "This morning when I got up, I forgot my foot was not there." Naturally, he fell to the cement floor face first. In the medical world, this is known as the phantom limb. In spite of his challenge, he always seemed to have a pleasant disposition and would laugh at himself. He usually had a smile on his face every day in class. Who would have thought that he was a dangerous felon?

The prison story was that he started with an abrasion from playing basketball. The sore soon turned into an infection on his foot that kept getting worse. While trying to seek medical attention, the problem was not treated properly and the infection advanced to the point where it was too late to for his foot to be saved. Because of the medical neglect, amputation was necessary. After realizing the gross claims that he could launch against the State, they talked him into a small settlement that seemed to make him happy. This incident was well before the medical departments in prisons took a turn for the better under court order.

It would stand to reason that a footless person who walked with a cane ought to be placed on the first floor of the housing unit. There were five housing units at Folsom and while they all had a first floor, some five-tiered units would have been a challenge for a physically impaired person to walk or climb because of the stairs. My student was typically on the 3rd tier. He didn't mind because it kept him close to his buddies. That was far more important that a few flights of stairs.

My questions: Who was paying attention? What would happen in an emergency? Could it lead to another law suit? Without up-to-date computers, how could the administration keep track? Was this done out of spite or revenge? I couldn't help but wonder. I had witnessed ugly things on many occasions that served no purpose but retribution. My training at the time of hire said, "These men are here for punishment. It is not up to you to punish them further." If it were necessary to discipline because of a rule violation, there was a progressive write up process. Everyone was trained in how to write the various degrees of disciplinary reports. Yet, some individuals willfully took matters into their own hands. The results of the latter were never helpful or productive.

During another year, I met a man without an arm. I don't know when he decided to have a happier disposition than the one he arrived with, but after four decades of incarceration, there he was—a happy, one-armed man. He would camp out on the main prison yard every day, rain or shine, and even during some lockdowns, and greeted everyone who passed. He never seemed to say anything negative to anyone, at least not to staff. He may have, I just never heard it. I often heard him chuckle at the younger prisoners and admonish, "You'll learn!" They probably reminded him of himself when he was at that age and stage of prison life—hard headed, defiant, and with ego and anger in the driver's seat.

Everyone got to know him by his nickname, Handy! Handy was part of the living institution of prison—the ghost of prison past, present, and future. With all of the years he spent in prison, and all of the things he witnessed and survived, his life story would be enough to set a youngster down and make them think twice.

Handy was not a student in Education, but everyone in Education and throughout the prison knew him. If they did not, it would not take long before they did. After several decades of incarceration, the word at the prison was that Handy finally got a date to parole and passed away before that date arrived. I imagine that just knowing he was going to leave was enough for him after all those years. That was the only adult life he knew. Prison was comfortable and familiar—a known quantity. The outside world was scary and different—an unknown domain.

After seeing Handy almost every day of my work life on the prison yard, he became as familiar as the other landmarks on the yard. Not seeing him stirred an empty feeling that made me ask myself, would I be able to make it out of the front gate alive? It was a reminder that nothing ever stays the same and that changes are always happening. In the almost 125 year history of Folsom State Prison, I could not begin to guess how many people, prisoners and staff, have died on that infamous yard. The signs posted on the yard read: "No Warning Shots Fired"—meaning, we shoot to kill. This was also a reminder to retire before I died on that yard. It was a relief when Folsom changed, and those "Shoot to Kill" signs came down.

In my early years, there was a man without sight. He had been declared legally blind. He was required to wear an orange vest so that he could be easily identified in the event of a problem on the main yard. The prison did not have any way of knowing some things without using that orange vest, but that's another story. The man who couldn't see loved to visit my classroom once or twice a week to borrow novels/stories on cassettes. He would listen to them back in his cell over and over, until he could return to Education to check out more.

Often a few of the lesser minded officers would stop him, give him a few spins in a circle, and then let him try to find his way. That may have been a good laugh and time killer for them, but this man just seemed to take it all in stride as he was never upset or unhappy by the time he reached my classroom. While it was distressing for me to hear of his account, he would say, "It's nothing." "Let them have their fun, I just want to get here for more cassettes."

Remembering this story triggered a memory of a time when an alarm was sounded in the Education Building. It was early in the morning before classes started and before many of the teachers arrived. I was on the yard heading to the building. I noticed that as several officers were running toward the Building, one officer tripped and fell to the asphalt. But, he bounced back up, took a second to observe who was around, and proceeded to run into the building.

The four prisoners standing against the outside wall of the school building all laughed. Once the officers determined it was a false alarm, they came out to take those four men away for laughing at the officer who fell. One of them was my clerk at the time, a young man of 21 who was still full of immature tendencies. I did not see him for about three months. When he returned, I learned that he had been moved to Corcoran State Prison and was in a cell not far from Charles Manson.

Knowing that this was the retaliatory climate at the time, I left the blind man's situation alone. There is no telling what his retribution would have been if those officers were reported and disciplined for their behavior. The blind man may have been shipped to another prison where the treatment could have been worse. Something told me that this blind man had already seen worse. Instead, he continued to enjoy the cassettes until I transferred to a different education program in a different building. Sometimes, all I could do was say a prayer. Most times, I held the whole prison in prayer that it would one day become a museum with the main yard being the park for picnicking families. One day!

Then, there was the man without an anus—no joke. He wore a colostomy bag and certainly had many challenges in the correctional system. It was noted in his file that he was not allowed to work around food, so the kitchen detail was off limits to him. One guess as to where he was assigned to work at Folsom? Yup, the kitchen! Most times, whenever a prisoner had anything to complain about, it was taken as whining and no one wanted to hear it. For some reason, the medical department would only issue one bag at a time, so that became an additional handicap in and of itself. Once the kitchen manager got tired of him dripping all over the place, he was assigned to education.

Yes, Education was often a collecting pool for those souls the institution did not know where else to place. Everything in prison was designed to be a limitation for both prisoners and staff. My limitation, or my blessing as this man's teacher, was to figure out a way to make it work. I soon found that he was just happy to have someone listen to his plight even though I was not in a position to do anything but to keep sending him to the medical office when the need arose.

Once a kind ear was available to listen, this student was delighted as this was a validation of him as a human being. Everyone wants to be validated, to know they have some worth and reason for being. This is the case from the warden to the most despicable prisoner. My feeling was that the behavior that led to prison needed to be changed in order for life to be viewed as more valuable. And, I had to be able to model the desired behavior for all students. This student settled into the routine and only came to me when he needed me to listen.

Modeling the desired behavior is nothing new for most conscientious families around the world. We want the young ones to learn from us how to behave and handle different situations. The younger they are, the more they remind me of a mound of dough ready for kneading into different shapes and designs based on who was working the dough. One never has to guess where the child's words or behaviors came from, just check out those in the environment. Yes, it was challenging to exercise patience with an adult as it was far easier to shout out, "Shut up, and sit down!" Patience was my practice and that lesson worked its way into a blessing on many occasions. Unconditional regard for life works in all cases.

Alas, I met a man with no ear! Wow, that was a fascinating first for me. Judging by his appearance, he was a skin head. Their bald tattooed heads were a dead give away! For some reason, I, who happened to be a woman of color, looked forward to working with those who declared themselves skin heads. Part of the enjoyment for me was to demonstrate that people of color were human beings just like them because there is only One Species--Humans. My attempt often failed because they would soon declare me different and therefore an exception to their rule. (I must be mixed with something with which they could identify.)

Even though the prison had more rules than anyone could ever count, the various groups in the prison also had their own set of rules that numbered more than anyone could count. Yet, survival meant that the rules had to be learned quickly either the easy way or the hard way which could result in pain or death.

The man without an ear was due to be released in less than two months. He eyed me for a couple of days before feeling comfortable enough to approach me to ask a question. Once at my desk, I was able to see close up that there was simply a hole in the side of his head with no trace of an outer ear lobe. The skin around the hole was smooth and unscarred. He had taken the liberty of having an ear lobe tattooed on his head around the hole. Having no hair seemed to accentuate everything about him. There didn't seem to be any hearing impairment. He quickly felt the need to explain that he lost his ear in a motorcycle accident. With motorcycle accidents, we all know he was fortunate to have only lost his ear.

We engaged in a conversation about employment options available to him once he paroled. Also, I was able to take a moment to explain the latest research I had read where medical science was now growing human noses and ears from grafted human cells onto the backs of pigs and mice. And, it could be worth it for him to investigate that avenue in the future. Those doing the experiments might be delighted to have a willing participant who needed a human ear. He was tickled and certainly left class with new information about his options and possibilities. I can only pray that those options would include humans of color. Many times the people we "rule" out of our lives are the very ones who have shown up to help us along our journey.

The happiest and funniest student I ever met had no physical disability at all. He loved making people laugh and once he discovered I loved to laugh, he considered my class heaven. People in prison hardly ever laughed unless they were laughing at someone else's misfortune. But, prison was too miserable to stay solemn all the time. So, we laughed a lot in my room.

It seemed that this student had part of his heart missing. Therefore, he needed to fill that space with something he could nurture and care for to fill that heart space. There were other prisoners who adopted feral cats, some caught lizards, and others caught birds to care for.

At one time I had about four or five green plants throughout the classroom. Mr. Green appointed himself the classroom gardener and would let me know when to bring more soil or plant food for "his babies." All leaves on the vines, Creeping Charley, and Elephant Ears were dusted and polished to a high gloss with only water and a paper towel. They all looked more vibrant and healthy than anything I had ever seen at a nursery. Mr. Green would even grow new plants from the pieces that broke. And, he would share some of the broken pieces with students to take and grow in their cells for a home-like atmosphere. All guests to the classroom noticed the plants right away and commented on how lovely the room looked with them.

Mr. Green would talk and sing to the plants as he tended to them. Those plants responded in kind as they were all vibrant. He also used the plants to send messages. One day, I called a student to my desk to discuss his inability to begin the assignment. He was distracting others and wasting time. Mr. Green was working on a plant nearby and before the student at my desk could explain himself, Mr. Green started singing, "I'm sorry...So sorry!" This broke the entire class out into laughter. The student at my desk rose and said, "I got the message Ms. C" and "I'll get busy." That was the end of it. I guess Mr. Green was also the self-appointed disciplinarian.

Many times my students, these grown men, felt they had a comfortable environment to let loose their anger. And, many times the disruption would happen while I was at the board trying to deliver a lesson. Who or what was not the issue, the potential for violence was always my concern. Therefore, I would immediately invite the person to step outside the classroom and to wait in the hallway. As they stomped to the door, Mr. Green's voice could be heard singing to the plants in the background, "I'm sorry...So sorry!" And for whatever reason, that song always stirred up laughter and brought down the level of tension that had crept into the room. It also calmed me down so I could effectively finish the lesson and deal with the situation waiting in the hallway. I came to call Mr. Green the "singing bouncer." His song was a constant reminder that a simple apology could make all the difference in most situations.

Thank you Mr. Green wherever you are!

Heart Lesson ~ I learn to keep an open mind over the situation at hand, whatever it may be. Being willing to do so in a positive way will reveal an even greater plan for my life!

View looking up to the Main Exercise Yard; Greystone Chapel on left; Housing Unit 1 on right. The space between the buildings, was called Blood Alley.

CHAPTER 5

Tricks of the Trade

The true science and study of man is man.
--Pierre Charron

Learning to be a teacher in prison was going to be the easy part. Learning the fine points of how to be a female working in a male dominated industry was going to take time, patience, and mentoring. There were no mentors around. Other teachers were too busy. Supervisors loved attending meetings and trainings. Therefore, it became a "figure it out as you go" way of doing things which takes patience. While I was trying to figure out how the prison operated, the prison officials were trying to figure out how to work with the influx of females in every position and program in the institution. Based on the number of harassment charges and millions of dollars in lost cases, the system was not doing too good.

I'll never forget during my second week of work at the prison, I entered the Education Building and was introduced to the personal alarms designed to be worn on your waist belt. The introduction was: "Put your chit in the drawer and take an alarm. Push the button if you need help," the Education Officer blurted out as if he was tired of having to repeat himself. I knew enough to not take it personally. I had spent most of the first two weeks on the job observing different classrooms at New and Old Folsom, therefore an alarm had not been necessary until now. My assignment was right here at Old Folsom.

I placed my shiny, brand new brass chit with my name etched on it in the drawer where the alarms were kept. The chit would let anyone know who had that alarm. The alarms were kept at the Education Officer's station. I laid the alarm on the counter while I unbuckled my belt. When I picked the alarm up to slide it on my belt, an ear piercing siren sounded and a glaring, bright, blue light on the wall-mounted alarm began to flash like the red lights on an ambulance.

The entry door to Education popped open and a group—perhaps eight to ten officers, with batons in hand, ran in and scattered throughout the building yelling as they went. Prisoners were dropping to the floor, people were hollering, "get down, get down." And, there I stood as frozen as a statue trying to figure out what the heck this was all about. I was still standing at the counter with the alarm in my hand watching and wondering if this was a movie, and someone had just yelled, "Action!"

Since I was the person front and center with an alarm in my hand, it was determined that somehow I had triggered this dastardly device. Soon, a sergeant shouted, "All Clear," and the alarm was turned off. Within minutes, everything went back to business as usual as if nothing had happened. Yet, there I stood wondering what happened, stunned that I had caused it to happen, and impressed over the rapid response.

I hadn't yet reached the part in my prison training where someone told me what to do when an alarm is sounded. Do I hit the floor or run for cover? Am I supposed to run around the building with the officers or stay put? I was mystified. After being laughed at for a couple of minutes by colleagues and officers, I was left alone to get over my embarrassment and to carry on with the business at hand. I still needed to get that alarm on my belt.

Once again, I picked up the alarm in an attempt to gingerly slide it onto my belt, and once again the alarm was triggered. Yikes! We had an instant replay with the officers storming back through the door, prisoners dropping to the floor and me standing there wondering what happened all over again. Between takes, no one had briefed me on anything so there I stood knowing that I somehow had done it again. But, what did I do? This is truly a learn-as-you-go place of employment. Was anyone going to help a Sistah out?

I looked down at my hand with the alarm in it to try to determine where I had gone wrong. Was I that stupid that I couldn't even get this simple device on without causing major disruptions? The alarm itself is a gadget similar to a garage door opener. It fits snuggly into a sturdy leather case with a hole for your finger to reach the alarm button. I noticed that as I cradled the alarm in the palm of my hand, my thumb was positioned above the hole for the alarm button. Then, I realized that the button was also above the hole and not positioned where it belonged. If I had not paid attention that time, there would have been a three-peat!

After the Sergeant cleared the alarm for the second time, he decided to stay with me until I had the alarm safely on my belt. I never found out if I got the "gag" alarm for new female employees or if I was just lucky enough to pick the flawed alarm. Right then, it did not matter. I decided to laugh right along with everyone else. It may have taken a couple of tries, but I nailed it on the third try, and I would not have to experience that again. Over the years I learned from the experiences of others so I wouldn't have to keep learning from my own embarrassing situations. This was a real "blue light" special I'll never forget.

Heart Lesson ~ Keeping a light and happy heart helps my heart stay healthy. Things in life don't have to be taken so seriously that it makes for unhappiness. I can have fun laughing at myself!

CHAPTER 6

The Magic Touch

The universe is full of magical things patiently waiting
for our wits to grow sharper. --Eden Phillpots

(Note: *This story was first published in CHICKEN SOUP*
FOR THE PRISONER'S SOUL, Health Communications,
Inc., Deerfield, FL, 2000, p.91. © Toni Carter)

Part of the satisfaction for any teacher is seeing the light go on when a student is able to grasp a new concept. It's no different for those of us who happen to teach incarcerated adults.

I used to constantly drill my seventh and eighth grade academic class on the merits of honesty when it came to taking tests. I would remind them that, "Cheaters never win, and winners never cheat." Many times this admonition would illicit boos and snickers, but I would repeat it anyway, and remind them that when they cheated, they weren't cheating me—only themselves.

As I sat grading a language test that required using simple, compound and complex sentences, I noticed that two of my adult inmate-student papers had the exact same sentences. I didn't intend to make a big scene out of it, so I simply wrote on each paper, "My, your answers are exactly the same as Mr. _____'s. When you decide to rely on your own intelligence, you will begin to amaze yourself." Once I made my comments and returned the papers to the class, I didn't give the incident another thought.

Moments after returning to my desk and beginning another stack of paperwork, an irate student jumped up from his desk in the full heat of anger. It took me a moment to realize what was going on and another moment to zero in on what he was saying. By then, he was at my desk hovering over me with his paper in hand. He not only had my attention, but the entire class was frozen in anticipation of what was going to happen next.

At our institution, all staff are required to carry whistles, and those working directly with inmates must wear personal alarms at all times. I could sense immediately that the rest of the class was waiting for me to push my alarm due to this impending threat of great bodily harm.

Once an alarm is sounded, within seconds, a full complement of custody officers is on hand to deal with the situation by whatever means is necessary. It's also understood that all inmates must stop where they are and either sit in their seats or on the floor if no seat is available. They must not in any way impede the movement of custody officers to the scene of the alarm.

Knowing this, my class became as quiet as those proverbial church mice. It was so quiet I could hear a heartbeat—mine! The entire situation seemed surreal and almost as though I was having an out-of-body experience. I listened to this middle-aged man's nonstop ranting.

Both he and I knew that all attention was squarely focused on us. All were waiting to see how this performance would play out. They already knew I would win because I automatically had the upper hand. But, what would winning cost me? A staff assault? Embarrassment? A shouting match? Humiliation and a weakened base of authority? Regardless, I was not prepared to pay the price. In a situation such as this, it's imperative to maintain control without compromising the trusting relationship I had built with the other students.

After reflecting on this student I thought I knew well, I looked at him with a smile, gently placed the palm of my hand under his chin and said, "Unclench those jaws before you talk to me, Mister." I didn't yell and it wasn't a threat. In an instant, the student melted into a stick of butter, and everyone was laughing, including him. In the next breath, he apologized and said he was sorry for yelling. Then he admitted cheating and felt bad for getting caught. He said, "Gee, Ms. Carter, not only did I get caught cheating, but then I had the nerve to make you prove it to me." He vowed never to do it again.

I could almost hear the whoosh of air as the other students breathed a sigh of relief. I could see the light of recognition in his eyes over the lesson he had just taught himself. All it took was a magic touch that transmitted more than I realized. It put everyone else "on notice" that I was for them—not against them.

> *He who learns but does not think, is lost! He who*
> *thinks but does not learn is in great danger.*
> **Confucius**

Epilogue

It takes courage to grow up and become who
you really are. --E.E. Cummings

During the early 1990's, Folsom State Prison changed its custody level from a Maximum Security prison to a Medium Security prison. This meant that several changes had to be made including moving all higher security prisoners to other prisons. This would make room for those ranked medium security. Good behavior allows a person to gradually lower their security level. The student in the above story was one of hundreds who had to be moved to another prison.

Sometime during 2003, as I walked through the housing unit to get to the main education building, I heard a voice calling my name. When I looked up, it was the very same student I had written the story about. He came down the stairs from the second tier and walked over to me with a big smile on his face. He asked, "Do you remember me?" Even though that incident happened about 12 years earlier, I remembered. He had reduced his points enough to be transferred back.

I shook his hand and said, "Not only do I remember you, I wrote a story about you!" He looked amazed and wanted to know what I meant. I told him I could show him better than I could tell him. So he followed me back to the classroom where I put a copy of the book in his hands. I said, "Have a seat and start reading."

As he read, his smile grew broader, and I could see him shake his head here and there. When he finished reading his first words were, "Over the years, I often thought of what I put you through. I knew I had to change my behavior, and I sure want to apologize again." I told him that he had a hard head, but deep down I could tell he had a kind heart. I said, "Do you know what hard heads make?"

He said, "I know, a soft behind."

I said, "No, at your age, a hard head makes a prisoner!"

He said, "Thanks for putting up with me, I'll never forget you."

We shook hands and he departed back into the prison wilderness. I never saw him again.

Heart Lesson ~ Overreacting feels like a plot by the ego to disrupt my life. The calm Peace of my soul is my desire regardless of appearances. In the peace of the Universe, I am always safe.

Note: *It was from the top of the stairs on the right that my former student called out to me. He came down the stairs and met me in the walk way.*

CHAPTER 7

The Stroke

None is more impoverished than the one who has no gratitude.
Gratitude is a currency that we can mint for ourselves, and spend
without fear of bankruptcy.--Fred De Witt Van Amburgh

There was a point where I could tell that this job that I enjoyed so much was taking a toll on me. Teaching 60 men at a time even with a teaching partner was a lot to handle. We had three weeks to prepare those who were paroling to understand what employment, housing, educational, and community resources were available. After 5, 10, 15 plus years in prison, three weeks was hardly enough preparation time, but that's all we had. We packed as much into the program as we could and then had two days to process the paper work that finished one class and to prepare the paperwork for the next 60. This pace went on for five years—nonstop. Our only breaks came with a week or two of vacation each year. Our school year was 365 days long with no program closure, least someone think that a State worker was loafing on the job.

One Saturday morning, I woke looking forward to celebrating my son's birthday. My intention was to shower, do a little housecleaning, place balloons and party decorations around the dining room, and take off for the restaurant about noontime. A protein smoothie seemed the easiest and fastest breakfast so I could move forward with the day. The smoothie went down easy, but seemed to hit my stomach like a brick of clay. A heavy, sleepy feeling slowly crept over me, and it seemed like the phone would not stop ringing.

I tried to shake off the feeling during the first call. It was a friend calling to say she would meet us at the restaurant. As soon as she heard my voice, she commented that I sounded funny. I tried to explain that I had a smoothie that was making me feel sluggish and making me feel as if I needed a nap. She said she would call back in 30 minutes. Before I could stand, the phone rang again. It was another friend calling to RSVP. She also commented about how there was a drunken quality in my voice. I tried to explain the green smoothie and all she could say was to call the advice nurse at the hospital for a possible antidote. She insisted and made me promise.

When I stood, I realized it was difficult to walk. I needed to get to my insurance card and the hospital phone number. As I stumbled into walls trying to make my way, I gave myself a pep talk: "Snap out of it, you can shake this off, you've got things to do today. Straighten up!" I was very upset with myself, and I would have gone back to bed if I hadn't promised my friend I would make this call. With all the energy I could muster, I got the phone number and my insurance card and staggered my way to the recliner in the living room.

This was a great relief—I was exhausted. Before I could dial the number, the phone rang again. This time it was my brother who immediately told me that I sounded loopy. Okay, this third call was definitely a warning that something was happening. I tried to explain to my brother about the smoothie and that I was about to call the advice nurse at the hospital. He asked me to call him back right after I made that call. I finally dialed the number.

Before I could completely explain what this dastardly smoothie was doing to me, the advice nurse said: "Oh, it sounds like you need to be here!"

Since everyone was telling me I sounded funny, I tried to carefully enunciate my words. I heard my startled voice respond: "Really? Well, let me hang up and call someone."

She said, "No, you just stay on the line and I'll call someone. Please don't hang up."

She was back on the phone in short order asking me questions that I tried to slowly and carefully explain. In what felt like seconds, I saw a fire engine pull up to the front of the house followed by a squad car and an ambulance. Everyone jumped out of their vehicles and ran to the door, banging as if they were about to tear the door down.

I explained to the nurse, they're here, and I have to go open the door. I was growing more and more emotional because I didn't feel like I needed all of this attention and commotion. Why couldn't she just give me a simple antidote: "drink warm milk; flush your system with water; suck on a lemon—there had to be something simpler than the emergency that was unfolding.

The nurse asked me if I could get to the door. It never occurred to me that I couldn't. But, when I tried to rock myself out of that chair, I felt like I was trying to lift dead weight. So, I decided to slide to the floor and crawl to the door. I was able to unlock and open the big door and sit there holding the screen door open. The problem was, in the time it took to get to the door, everyone was up the driveway at the back door.

I saw someone running down the driveway to the fire truck, and he glanced over and saw me. Within seconds everyone was in the living room with a gurney. An EMT asked me if I could make a fist. There I sat on the floor with my legs stretched out in front of me. I was looking at my hands telling myself to make a fist. Nothing happened. I thought, how curious that I can't make a fist.

"Wiggle your toes." Again, I tried, but to no avail. I was stumped! What on earth was happening to me?

In the next second, I was hoisted onto the gurney. I heard someone go to the phone and say to the nurse, "We got her and are on the way."

As soon as he hung up, the phone rang. It was my brother checking back. The officer let him know that they were loading me into the ambulance and were heading to the hospital. That was great timing.

Being in law enforcement, my brother was ready for emergencies although I don't think he ever expected his sister to be one of those emergencies. As soon as he learned the situation, he decided to come by the house to be sure it had been locked and secured. He arrived at the house the same time my son pulled up. He caught him up on what had happened and together they secured the house and headed to the hospital.

I had never been in an ambulance before. While the EMT tried to hook up an IV, that dang smoothie decided to exit. The EMT grabbed my sweat shirt and rolled me over in time for me to make a mess all over him and the floor. I must have emptied all 20 ounces of that green drink. Yikes! What an embarrassing mess. And then, I was in the emergency room. I didn't blank out, I just live that close.

I had no way of knowing, but the emergency room seemed empty. I was taken in for a CAT scan. Afterwards, the doctor came in and said, "I guess you know you've had a stroke, and you are very lucky to have survived." So, that was it! I felt so clueless. I guess I ought to have known, but I didn't. In my case, I think ignorance was bliss. I did not know what to panic about. Then the doctor stated that there was evidence in the scan of a previous stroke! What? Without invitation, my mind dashed back several months to me standing at the podium in front of the classroom. I was discussing something with the class and remember feeling woozy to the point of needing to hold onto the podium to steady myself. I thought, gee I'm tired and hope break time arrives soon. That must have been a small something happening to me then.

When the doctor left my side, I looked at the clock, 11:30 am—still time to make the birthday luncheon. Then, I heard the doctor on the other side of the curtain letting my brother and my son know that I had to be admitted. That's when it really sunk in that was a game changer. The doctor said, "She can't even walk so we can't let her go like this."

It took about three hours before I was wheeled to a room. I had the space by the window. As I stared out the window, I prayed: God, I am not able to get to what I need to heal, so thank you for bringing it to me. Then, I resigned myself to get on with healing. Interestingly enough, a RN came into the room and performed acupressure on the toes of my paralyzed side—the right, saying that the stroke occurred in my left brain. Then she showed my brother how to do it, and he took over for several minutes.

The nurse returned to tell me I had so many visitors in the hallway that she was going to move me to the larger room with a single bed tomorrow. I had no idea who was in the hallway as I only got to see my brother and my son that evening. But, just as promised, about noontime the following day, Sunday, I was moved to a corner room at the end of the hallway. Wow! There was plenty of privacy, plenty of sunlight, and plenty of space!

I remember laying there reflecting on how I always said that when it is my time to go, I want to peace out. The stroke was peaceful with no pain attached. It was just a slow and gradual loss of everything from the ability to swallow, move, speak, or breathe in a normal manner. I am now extremely mindful of what I tell myself. Then the words of comedian Redd Foxx crept into my mind, "You're gonna feel mighty stupid lying in the hospital bed dying from nothing." Meaning, it's going to be something for each one of us on that appointed day. I also heard Caroline Myss, Medical Intuit and Author, say that most people aren't afraid to die, they are afraid of how they are going to die. But, I can assure you that death was not on my mind. Only healing!

By the next day, I had severe ringing in my ears that was non-stop. To add a little more to the hodgepodge of maladies, I was experiencing quadruple vision. I remember a doctor coming into the room to check on me. When he asked how I was doing, I commented about what a lucky person because I was to be able to see "4" of my favorite people all at once. I'm sure he thought I had lost a part of my mind. It wasn't until the middle of the second week in the hospital that my friend Helen made a connection to the daily heparin (blood thinner) shots. While this was not supposed to be one of the side effects, it certainly was for me. As soon as the shots stopped, so did the ringing in my ears.

Also on the second day of hospitalization, Helen brought a lady who was a licensed physical therapist. Sue had gone for a specialized training in a technique called, Integrative Manual Therapy (IMT). Quite simply, this technique works to open energy blockages in the body. It worked to help me significantly move into the healing process much faster. Sue worked on me for about four days during the first week. By the time she finished, I could swallow and be taken off the IV. No one at the hospital knew or understood what was going on behind the curtain in my room. Their objective was to free up that bed as soon as possible for the next patient. But, Sue and her abilities allowed me to advance to the world of pureed foods.

Additionally at the end of the week, I couldn't believe how my room had filled with flowers, gifts, balloons, stuffed animals, and cards from all over. Even the men in the Life Forum and a few of my students managed to get a few things in to me to let me know they were all praying for me.

I was getting well wishes from people that I didn't even realize knew me. One gift from my teaching partner was a cloth covered sponge ball. My right arm was kept propped up on a pillow. On the day he brought the ball, he lifted my hand and put the ball underneath. He simply said, "Work with that." Well, I would have if I could have. Once the nurse saw it, she immediately removed it saying it could interfere with my therapy by using the wrong muscle groups. What?! Didn't she know I'd be happy to move any muscles? Whenever a visitor came into the room, I would have them find that ball and put it back under my hand. The nurse and I played this game for a few days.

As life would have it, I stayed hospitalized a second week while waiting bed space at the Rehabilitation Facility in Vallejo, CA. As I lay in the hospital bed in the midst of waking one morning, I felt two fingers on my right hand squeeze the ball! I instantly knew that was the beginning of the physical journey back. The next day, a nurse came in to bathe me and decided I ought to do it myself. She handed me a warm, moist cloth. Using my left hand, I was able to sponge off my face and arms. Just as I was about to reach for my right leg, it flew up in the air as if on a puppet's string. I was startled as it felt like an involuntary action. I looked at the nurse and said, "I'm scared of me!" We both smiled and went on with the sponge bath.

By departure time for Vallejo, I was using a walker to navigate the hallway. Upon arrival at the Rehabilitation Center, I was asked what my goal was. I told them I had three goals: 1) bathe myself; 2) dress myself; 3) walk out unassisted by the end of my two week stay. The doctor simply said, "We are here to help you meet those goals." That's all I needed to hear, as my heart already knew it was possible. I wanted all interested parties on the same bandwagon.

My days were busy from sun up to sun down. We started with breakfast and then an occupational therapist came in to help me dress since I was unable. It took time, but somehow I was able to put on all articles of clothing except my bra, so I tried to get away without it—didn't need it. Once the occupational therapist caught on to my omission, she insisted that I wear it every day. I was in no position to fight that battle so I struggled with that contraption until I mastered it.

If it were shower day, there was a nurse assistant to roll you into the shower before dressing. Then you had to get into your wheel chair and get to your designated area. For me, it was the gym for two sessions with two different physical therapists. Then it was off to the cafeteria for lunch. There was a brief rest period back in the room before over to a different wing for occupational and specialized therapy. After another little respite, we were back to the cafeteria for dinner. The dinner hour was followed by activities in the game room where you could play bingo or other games, and even watch a video. By 9 pm, everyone was rolling back to their rooms for the evening.

The entire experience was filled with sweet memories. On one day in particular, I was attempting my first try at navigating in a wheel chair to the dining hall. Anyone could request their meal in their room. Each room had four patients. But, everyone was encouraged to join others for the benefits of socialization. I was there to do the best I could with everything assigned. However, it was a tad frustrating to be in a wheelchair for the first time and only be able to go in circles. I still had no strength in my right side and could only use my left hand to steer.

As I sat in that extra wide hallway trying to figure out this dilemma, Bernice, a 400 pound lady in a motorized cart stopped and said, "You look like you could use a lift! Slip your hand in the back pocket of my chair and you can ride with me." Problem solved!

Bernice drove me straight to the dining room and up to a table. There were no chairs in this dining room as everyone came by way of wheel chair. Bernice explained that until they could make a wheel chair to accommodate her size, she was allowed to use her personal motorized chair. For the rest of the first week, Bernice met me in my room to give me a lift for all meals. By the second week, I had gained enough strength to wheel the chair on my own using both arms.

Part of the specialized physical therapy training included muscle memory exercises. The therapists would move my arm mimicking normal arm movements to remind the muscles of how they are supposed to respond. They also worked my leg in the same manner. My arm and leg seemed to be ready to remember. I always welcomed these routines because each session got me closer to full recovery. Towards the end of the second week, I was bathing myself, dressing myself, and walking with a four-pronged cane. On the day I left, I did not need it at all. I was encouraged to take the walker, but everything else stayed behind.

Three weeks later, I had my first out-patient physical therapy appointment at the clinic near home. When I walked in, the therapist said, "I remember you from the hospital. I can't believe you walked in here without a cane." And for that very reason, they deemed me unsuitable for any further outpatient therapy. They only wanted to get me to the point of being able to walk with a came. Thank goodness I wanted more for myself. All other therapy I did on my own. I was able to return to work after three months. I promised myself I would slow my pace and take better care of myself mentally, emotionally, physically, and spiritually. My priority was me.

A big part of my healing was being open to the love that flowed in from all directions. The men in my class as well as the men from the main prison yard in general had found ways to send me cards, prayers, and well wishes. The night after I dreamt of holding a teddy bear, a friend walked in with a giant teddy bear. My brother and son visited every evening to be sure I had a good belly laugh for the day. Between the two of them, I laughed until I cried on top and on the bottom which kept the nursing assistants busy changing sheets. All the nurses marveled over the gifts and flowers that arrived daily. The visitors were too numerous to mention, but in time I thanked each and every one of them. My spiritual community held me tight in prayer. The energy of love binds us and heals us. I was enveloped in love and will forever be grateful!

Heart Lesson ~ Every act of kindness is an act of love and a heart conditioning to the giver as well as the receiver. I commit to committing acts of love every day.

CHAPTER 8

Love It or Fear It

*When there is no enemy within, the enemies outside
cannot hurt you. --African Proverb*

Somewhere along my path in life, I had to make up my mind I was not going to live in fear. I spent many of my young years afraid of snakes, afraid of the dark, afraid of the neighborhood bully, afraid of going to high school—just plain afraid of too many things. While I still would prefer not to come across a snake, the rest of those fears have been left far behind.

By the time I started working at Folsom State Prison, I had already taught for a couple of years in the Detroit Public School System. Cooley High School reminded me of the high school I graduated from in New Jersey. It was a massive building that covered a couple of blocks and was filled with thousands of students. Our graduating class alone was 1,000 students. One could easily get lost in such a grand maze. Cooley High School felt like a replica of my high school. My daily roster contained 5 classes of 35 students assigned to each class. Of course, I never saw half of the students as most regularly skipped class. I refused to pass a student that I never saw.

However, this is where I learned about weapon sweeps and gang activities that spilled in from the streets—drug sales, fights, prostitution, and perhaps other things that were better left unmentioned. Teachers parked their cars in a lot that was locked by 8 a.m. and unlocked at the end of the school day. The few security officers on staff were needed inside building and not out in the parking lot watching our cars. In my short tenure there, a few cars were stolen that did not make the locked lot in time. Looking at things from a thug mentality, what a wonderful place to steal cars, sell drugs and do what we want, it's all concentrated in one area. This was their market place!

It didn't take long for this new teacher in prison to feel at home. In fact, teaching in prison was more to my liking as students were required to attend class, and they were adults—at least in age. As we enjoy this human experience for the span of a lifetime, it is good to know that it is that Infinite Spirit that unites us in breath and views us all One. Our differences reveal how magnificently diverse we all are. People have a right to enjoy their own pursuit of happiness as long as it doesn't impinge on the rights of others. I wanted and needed to connect to that part in all of my students which is the same—that spiritual center—our unifying force.

I thought I was doing great with making those connections for increased motivation and learning to happen. Then one day, life brought me one of those special students that would take a little more time and effort. The dead giveaway was the Swastika tattooed in the middle of his forehead. As an African American, I smiled because I knew he was coming from a fearful place. He had a bit of a Charles Manson look about him for which he seemed to be proud. He entered the room in an agitated state demanding to know why he was assigned to school. "I'm crazy, and I don't belong in school," he shouted as he continued to prance back and forth in front of my desk. I asked him to be seated. I told him I would talk with him about his concerns as soon as I finished attendance.

He took a seat but quickly stood up, hesitated for a few seconds, and then continued shouting and prancing. Again I asked him to please be seated for a few moments. Attendance, which is another form of institutional head count, was the most important activity at that moment. The Education Custody Officer was waiting to find out if anyone was truant so he'd know if a search was necessary. My new student was too impatient to understand that or anything else. "I'm crazy, I don't belong here, call the psych—he'll tell you," he yelled out to the room. I guess he was used to getting his way. Everyone else in the room wanted to see what level of crazy he was going to display.

Hearing his words instantly reminded me of a previous student who had attended my class a couple of years prior. This student had regular visits with the institutional psychiatrist. One day he came to class chuckling to himself. I asked him to let me in on the joke. He said on his last visit to the Psych, the Psych asked if he heard voices. My student responded, "Yes, I do!" When asked what the voices were saying to him, he answered, "I don't know because they are speaking in a different language." They both had a good laugh. Yet, it made me wonder who's analyzing who? The more pressing question at this moment was--what was this current student hearing? It certainly wasn't me.

I left that reflection and returned to the whirl of activity as students were arriving so I could mark their attendance. They all took their seats, but young "Charlie" who still did not want to cooperate. I decided he had to calm down right now or chaos would soon come crashing in on us. Thus, I slipped into a moment of insanity myself. I jumped up from behind my desk, and with the meanest mug I could muster, I shouted, "We're all crazy in here, so sit down and don't move again until I call you!"

Young Charlie was as startled as the rest of the class. They all gave me that attentive deer in headlights glance. Charlie quickly took a seat and began to look around the room as if trying to detect insanity on the face of others. As he eyed those around him, it gave me a few extra moments to finish attendance and call the absentees to the officer. Young Charlie may have been thinking that perhaps he was in the right place after all. It was amazing that I never had to say another thing to him.

When I called Charlie to the desk for orientation, he nodded in agreement with everything I said. I was surprised that his argumentative position had changed so quickly. He returned to his seat and started on the assignment. He learned right away that I was not his enemy. I recognized the fear in him was spilling out as anger. Where else in the prison could he sit with an assortment of ethnicities comfortably?

Somehow he surmised that this was a safe place. He could have a chance to breathe, relax, and try to learn something. He really wanted to be in class as it was to his benefit. All who attend a program or work assignment everyday were entitled to "day for day" credit to reduce their sentence. I gathered that Young Charlie just wanted to know he would be accepted. As it turned out, he found others in class he could work with, and he soon became one of the best students in class. He completed his work in a timely fashion, and he did very well on all tests. I'm happy to report that he went on to successfully complete his GED.

Heart Lesson ~ My appearance and personality may be different from others, but in the eyes of the Infinite, we are all ingredients in the whole enchilada. And, what am I here for if not to be a beacon of light for others. Remembering this makes my heart sing.

CHAPTER 9

Gang Affiliated

*Discontent, blaming, complaining, self-pity cannot
serve as a foundation for a good future, no matter
how much effort you make. --Eckhart Tolle*

There was always a Draconian appearance and feel to Folsom State Prison and the rainy, misty, foggy days made it even more gloomy and depressing. I half way expected gargoyles to circle over head as we crossed the yard on the way to the Education Building in the early morning hours. The route always took us pass the room where the executions were carried out a century ago. The words "Death Row" were still painted above the doorway as our daily reminder. And, to make it even more interesting, there were plenty of puddles everyone had to dance around on the way. This was dismal for me so I knew it had to be even worse for my students who had to live that drama every day. The sunny work days were a Godsend.

Perhaps it was for these reasons that I put forth extra effort to be more patient and understanding of staff and students alike. Students detected my patience and kindness instantly and often tried to use it as the doorway to getting their wants satisfied. I could not afford to have them take advantage of my kindness as that ultimately would lead to full scale manipulation. Therefore, I worked to be even handed to each and everyone. When I wouldn't give in, some became annoyed. Their annoyance led me to my teacher's bag of tricks to create a distraction. Yes, parents do this with their toddlers and here I was doing the same with adults stuck in toddler mentality—go figure. At the time, teachers worked 10 hour days for four days a week, nine of those hours with students. Everyone knew that nine hours a day with students was a trying situation even for the best.

During the early mid-1990s, the Education Program had an extensive video library that included the Nova and National Geographic series, approved feature films and documentaries, and academic subject-related films. A video would often be a pick-me-up and a needed distraction on the dreary days. Students could look forward to a little entertainment while they were learning. And, this teacher could look forward to a little paperwork time while my nerves got a break.

I had been having a problem with two students who boasted of being members of a certain well-known gang whose name will remain anonymous. They refused to do any work and were trying their best to keep others from getting work done. They wore their pants so low; I couldn't imagine how they were staying up. If they could only understand how ridiculous they looked, they would stop. Sagging pants in prison was often a way to solicit a romantic interest. It let others know your were available. I don't know what it meant to these two other than a dedication to their lifestyle. My best motivational and rainy day techniques fell on deaf ears as these two were neither ready nor willing to cooperate at all.

Once I understood that my attempts to encourage had failed, the time had come for me to make a point. After all, these were two adults who kept insisting they were "men." They mentioned it every day. When I checked, my patience had expired, and now it was time for disciplinary action. I wrote both of them a warning. The second write-up would be a little sterner, and the third disciplinary action would request removal from the program.

All students understood that the progressive disciplinary process would mean copies sent to counselors, the disciplinary officer in their building, and it would become a permanent record in their main file. Possible removal from any work program meant a forfeiture of privileges and cell confinement. Cell or "C" status meant no leaving that cell for anything other than an emergency. The disciplinary officer determined the length of C-Status. Most prisoners tried to avoid these measures as it ultimately could add time to their sentence. For a decided few, it just didn't matter. These two students fell into the "it just didn't matter" category.

On the day that these men received their write ups, they were not happy about it. I had hoped the write-up would snap them into better behavior. It snapped them alright, but into the opposite direction. They confronted me on the matter, and I told them that if they could "dish" it out like men, then they had to be able to take it like men! My comment only added fuel to the slow burning fire that began to rage in them. Little did I know that they were plotting their revenge all morning. Revenge was their personal prison, and they were on a one-way road to misery.

We had in-class lunch at 11:30 a.m. and after eating, I went to the restroom. When I returned to the class, I noticed the room was unusually quiet. Everyone was acting as if they were busy working on an assignment. I knew it was too good to be true, but I had no idea what it meant so I just decided to be seated and enjoy the moment. The moment lasted a few seconds because as soon as I sat, I noticed something else was not right. My rain coat was draped over the back of the chair so I did not sit squarely on the seat. I did not notice anything on the seat before I sat.

As I sat, I could feel that my pants were snagged on something in the seat. When I tried to shift in the seat, I could feel a small tug. I put my hand behind me to see if I could feel what may have been causing the snag. The class stayed in complete silence. My little dumplings sure knew how to give themselves away without even trying. I had a sense that I was about to discover why.

With my hand behind me, I could feel an object protruding through the fabric cushion of the chair. I pulled it out and discretely held it under the desk to see what it was. Someone had opened a large paper clip, filed one end to a sharp point, and wove it into the seat cushion in hopes that I would plop down on it. Thank goodness the rain coat over the back of my chair kept me from sitting down on the full seat. Without looking surprised or saying a word, I left the room.

The education supervisor happened to be a few feet away talking to another teacher in the hallway. I waited patiently for him to finish while keeping an eye on my classroom door. Without fail, both gang members came to peer out of the small rectangular glass in the door. Each one darted away when they saw me standing there staring back at them. I'm not a detective, but even I could figure this one out.

Once the supervisor was free, I described what had just happened. Mr. D was normally a good natured person who reminded me of Captain Kangaroo. In this situation, he seemed to act like a Keystone Cop. He hemmed and hawed as if he did not know what to do. He wanted to pass it off as nothing, but decided that we should at least mention it to the Education Officer. Again I was getting a strong feeling that the prison was still trying to come to grips with females working in the prison. My guess is that a man may have handled the incident differently.

As soon as the Education Officer heard my account of the incident, he let us know that this was viewed as a staff assault, and that my entire class was going to be hauled out for interrogation. He called the Custody Complex and a host of officers were immediately present to escort my class over to the Captain's Office where they would be interviewed one at a time. The class had no idea what was going on, but when the officers burst into the room and told them to leave everything and stand immediately, they knew it wasn't going to be good.

As soon as the room was cleared, the Security & Investigation (S&I) officers, aka the Goon Squad, took my account of what happened and suggested that I report to the medical clinic to be sure I was alright. They cautioned me that there could have been something on the end of that needle point and if the skin was broken, I would be exposed to a variety of infections. Even with my assurances that I was fine, I still had to go so that an official report could be filed. I appreciated the thoroughness.

As I crossed the main yard to walk over to Medical, I had to walk by the area where my students were seated outside. Some of them yelled over asking if I was alright. I nodded yes and kept walking. I think those who did not know were just learning what had actually happened. I sensed that there may have been some students who were upset enough to take the investigation into their own hands to dish out their own form of prison justice. I did not want that to happen.

Once the medical personnel were satisfied that I was fine, there was an Employee Counselor standing by to interview me. He assured me they were going to take care of the situation and wanted to know if I was emotionally okay to go back to the classroom. Wow! What a great gesture this was! I so appreciated all the steps that were being taken to look after my safety. I was overwhelmed that this incident was being screened to such an intense degree.

While sitting on the examination table, my mind raced back to a time 15 years earlier when I sold real estate in Los Angeles. A prospective client pulled a gun on me and robbed the house I was showing. Thank goodness all he wanted was money and stuff. I was locked in a room until he was gone. When I got back to the real estate office, the broker offered me a couple of shots from a bottle of bourbon, and that was the extent of that episode. Now prison officials were actually demonstrating a concern. This incident proved to be a day and night difference. The human comfort and support did not compare to the comfort and support from a bottle of whiskey. Thank you Folsom State Prison.

When I got back to my classroom, S & I came back to let me know the results of their investigation. They mentioned that the class would not be coming back that day and possibly not the next day. They were all locked down and were told to think things over. The officers let me know that the only two students who felt like I deserved what I got were the two I suspected. The rest of the students were upset that it happened and told the Captain that I was a person who was really there trying to help them learn.

Before S & I finished speaking with me, the Captain was on the phone. He mentioned that it was obvious that the two culprits were not going to confess, and no one else claimed to have seen anything. He said they were two "bad eggs", and I should do another disciplinary report and send it directly to him so he could officially remove them from the class permanently before they had an opportunity to do real harm.

It was easy to write another disciplinary indicating that these two students would not cooperate with school rules. They refused to follow directions for completing class work or for maintaining proper grooming standards. They wore their pants closer to their knees than their waists. For those absolutely bent on hanging themselves, they will always find the rope to do it.

When my class returned two days later, those two men were not present. Ultimately, their misery took them to security cells in different prisons. The rest of the class seemed more relieved than I and wanted to know what took me so long to remove them. At last, we were able to put that gloomy day behind us and get back to the business of learning.

Throughout this situation and others, I always felt divinely protected. This is why I was not afraid to keep on teaching and keep on working to make learning a happy experience until I was able to retire on my terms.

Heart Lesson ~ I can forgive others for trespassing against me. I can love them from afar with grace and ease. My heart is not burdened by anyone's shadow.

CHAPTER 10

Suicide Watch

You cannot keep dancing with the devil and wondering
why you are still in hell. --Anonymous

The pressures and stresses of life, along with the pressures and stresses of working in a prison, can help one to develop a strong abiding faith in a higher power and learn to seek refuge there when times turn rough. So far, it's the only thing that personally sees me through, and I suspect always will. Today, a custody officer announced to the world that he wanted to literally flee to a different place by committing suicide! He wasn't the first to commit the deed, but he was the first to my knowledge to do it inside the prison walls. Other staff members have lost their lives on prison grounds, but at the hands of others.

Just a few months earlier, this particular officer notarized a document for me. He certainly was an amiable person and always seemed to be of good cheer. Just goes to show you that appearances can be deceiving. What wasn't deceiving was the fact that this individual was in a tower above Blood Alley in close proximity to the Education Building. Blood Alley got its name from all of the frequent stabbings and shootings that happened over the decades. That little stretch of yard, not even a block long, was so notorious that I'm sure prisoners heard about it before they arrived at Folsom.

On the yard, only officers assigned to towers carry guns. Officers on the ground have a variety of other deterrents at their disposal. Neither staff nor prisoners were allowed on the yard while the guns or ammunition were being raised to the towers. During the late 90s, there were large metal signs on the side of the buildings which indicated that NO WARNING shots would be fired. If an officer had cause to fire his weapon, it would be to shoot a perpetrator—center mass.

The signs alone gave me plenty of opportunity to pray without ceasing as I had to cross that yard and Blood Alley at least twice a day and sometimes more. This is why it was important not to wear anything that could be mistaken for prisoner clothing--not even the color blue— and to pray that whomever was holding that gun had excellent eye sight.

Officer Smith was in the tower on the top corner of a building that overlooked the main yard from one angle, and the other angle overlooked Blood Alley and the entrance door to Main Education. Of course there were plenty of other officers assigned to the yard itself so that all areas were covered. On this sunny afternoon, the yard was called in at approximately 3:30 p.m. Just as the men were heading in to their housing units, someone thought they heard a noise which sounded like a muffled gun shot. On first glance, there was nothing out of order. After the yard had cleared, an officer noticed blood dripping down the side of the building from the officer's tower. It was easy to figure out the rest.

At that point all gates were frozen, and a fire truck and investigative team were called in. No one would be moving for a long while. The prison officials couldn't even move Officer Smith until the preliminary investigation was complete. As the Education Building was right in the line of action, staff and students were sequestered until further notice. The only view of the yard from inside our building was through a small window in the main door. This window became off limits to all students. After being detained for two hours, I did get a chance to peep out the window. Just as I did, I watched a shroud covered gurney being lowered onto the fire truck's lift for removal.

I figured it couldn't be much longer. The ten hour day had stretched into 12 hours, and the students were beyond anxious. Once they learned what happened, they were beyond upset. It was disturbing to know that someone who had a gun trained on them as they moved on the yard could be loose cannon in their minds. How were these people being trained? Did they have to pass a psychological evaluation? What would keep them from firing on us when they had a bad day? Who was that officer? I had to remind my students that I had been in class with them all day and that I, too, had to move about on that yard every day.

A short while later, a plan had been devised to dismiss students out of the front door and through a tarp covered walkway that would allow them to enter the back of their housing unit. They would not be walking through the investigation area, nor would they be able to see the area. I collected my things and felt that soon we would be cleared to depart. I was not prepared for what happened next.

Staff was asked to convene in the middle classroom to talk to the trauma team. The middle room was the largest, but there was no classroom that would have been suitable for me after more than 13 hours of duty. Home was the only place I wanted to be. The trauma team consisted of two to three prison staff who had been through some type of training. While I can appreciate what they were trying to do, it did not work. I was more traumatized after the next hour of being with the trauma team than over the incident itself. This team picked and pried at everyone's emotions and did little in return to ease tensions. I couldn't believe how upset I was becoming. I tried my best to work it off on the way home. It wasn't easy.

I feel that this life is a gift, and I recognize that suicide, as everything else in life, is a choice. Officer Smith had to be feeling overwhelmed with the events of his life and decided to seek what he felt was a permanent resolution. There are several schools of thought on the subject of suicide. I am comfortable with the thought that death is not permanent as our soul's life is eternal. We do get to come back to have life in the physical many times.

There is now recorded documentation from individuals who can remember other lifetimes. Every day and in every event, we get to choose our behavior and attitude on this physical journey. We can lighten up and enjoy the ride knowing that stuff is going to happen. Or, we can decide that life is out to get us and make us miserable. We can't decide another person's happiness—it's a do-it-yourself operation. I knew this would be the discussion at the next meeting of my class.

The other teachers weren't ready to discuss the matter any further after the trauma team finished with us. We all had the same thing in mind—getting out of prison. Our watch was over. We didn't want to pass go, and we didn't want to collect $200, and we didn't want any more of the trauma team. Prison had monopolized more than enough of the day for all of us. As professionals, we were not entitled to overtime. And by the time I got home, there was only eight hours left for dinner and sleep before having to get up and do it all over again.

I wished they had given us a choice. Those interested in sitting with the trauma team would be able to have that time to discuss their feelings. The ones who felt they needed it would have benefited far more than forcing all of us to stay. But, we were under the prison's control and they always had the right of way. Perhaps taking his own life on grounds was Officer Smith's way of saying to the prison and the world that he got to make this decision of how he ended his own life. Perhaps, he felt in control for once.

As a final note, all staff is made aware of the "Employee Assistance Program" as an employee benefit. Many staff members that I have spoken to don't trust the program. They felt that it, like many other situations, was designed to get you to share private information so administrators could have grounds to be in the know for retaliation or firing. That's what stress will do to a person—make you paranoid of everything. In fact, most of us did not use the word paranoia. Instead we used the term "real-anoia."

Heart Lesson ~ While I don't claim to understand suicide or another person's journey in this life, I can work to keep my mind healthy and happy. Hopefully, my attitude will be an inspiration to others.

There are two raised towers on the left building, one at each corner. The far tower was the scene of the suicide. The fire engine was able to pull right into the road way.

CHAPTER 11

In The Dark

The dark is generous, and it is patient, and it always
wins. --Matthew Woodring Stover

On the four day a week work schedule, the teachers were getting up in the dark and getting home close to dark. It was always amusing to note how things were revealed in the light of day and even more interesting to note what those things were. I'm sure many people have had similar or even worse experiences. I only hope you were able enjoy a good belly laugh—I sure did.

On a chilly November day while standing out in the break area with my class, a student eased his way over, leaned in and whispered, "Are you alright today Ms. C?" I answered, "Yes, I'm fine, thank you."

This was not enough so he leaned toward me again and asked in a hushed voice, "You didn't have any problems getting out of the house this morning?" With a wrinkle in my brow I stated, "No, I was able to leave the house just fine." Again, he leaned in and asked: "Are you sure you didn't have to leave home in a hurry." I responded sternly, "NO! Why are you asking?" With a smile on his face he stated, "Because your socks don't match!"

With that, I looked down to see that I had on a brown sock and navy sock. In the dark they both looked brown to me! We both had a good laugh, and I made a point to check my entire appearance more carefully before leaving home. That certainly let me know that my students were checking me out and making certain assumptions about me and my home life.

Throughout the years, the practice of carefully scrutinizing staff, especially the females, never stopped. In earlier institutional trainings, we were told that these men will dress and undress you with their eyes. I'd like to think that because of my age and my size, there was no appeal when it came to me. I worked to cultivate a healthy level of respect and a reputation for fairness. But, what did I know?

I did not have long to laugh at myself because a month later, a teacher that I shared a classroom with told me that she felt funny when she came in that morning. As she was walking down the roadway, it was hard to keep her balance as she was wobbling. She told herself that something must be going wrong with her hip surgery and she would have to go get checked out. When she got to the classroom and took off her coat, she noticed one shoe was a flat and the other was a short pump! The day to day grind in prison was taking its toll on all of us.

Another teacher said she was at the board discussing a math lesson. She went to put her hands in her pockets while talking, and after fumbling with her pockets for several minutes, she became aware that her hands just would not go in. When she looked down, she realized she had her pants on backwards. That front zipper was supposed to be in the back. There was no more teaching that day. Thank goodness we can laugh at our human selves in those moments.

It wasn't so laughable when one day I accused my class of stealing a little battery operated keyboard. During my time of teaching literacy on computers, there were only 12 computers for my class of 24. When students were not on the computer, they could check out a keyboard and typing book and practice their keyboarding skills. By the end of one particular day, there was one keyboard missing. I had no idea when it went missing so by now, if someone really wanted it, it was probably already out the front door. Don't ask, because these students had ways I knew nothing about!

I had the discussion with the class that I wanted the keyboard back, and if it were returned before departure time, there would be no questions asked. If it were not returned, I had no choice but to have the officer come in to strip each student to find it. I guess you could say I was a tad upset that my students would steal from me even though several had been incarcerated for theft. I could hear them talking among themselves and encouraging whoever took it, to return it. No one budged!

I had already phoned the officer to inform him of the situation. My students heard me say, "Strip 'em out" so they would know I was serious. Plus, I wanted to send the message that thievery in this class was not going to work. At dismissal, the education officer held my class back, and another officer from the yard came in to help. Each student in my class had to remove all clothing down to their skivvies! I found a place out of the way in the teacher's room until the process was over. Of course, the keyboard was nowhere to be found.

When my students returned the next day they eagerly asked if the keyboard showed up. I shook my head with a disappointed look on my face. One student commented, "I don't think anyone here would steal from you, Ms. C." I smiled and said, "I sure hope you're right." I admonished myself for not being more careful. Staff had to be responsible for State Property because it was State Property, but more importantly, anything could be converted into a weapon and used for harm. I pushed the matter out of my mind and proceeded on with the work of the day.

As soon lunch time rolled around, students took out their brown bags and sat for lunch before going out to the break yard. That's when the door flung opened and in walked the teacher from the classroom next door with a keyboard in her hand. She promptly said, "Thank you Ms. C for lending me this keyboard! It's a fascinating little gadget and I think I'll order some for my class."

Oh my! I felt my face instantly turned to that deep shade of red that could fry bacon and eggs! It all came back to mind that a student from Mrs. Parker's class came over and said, "My teacher would like to borrow one of those things." He pointed to a keyboard that was on my desk. He wasn't going to fool me into just handing him a keyboard and then disappearing. I had about eight years of working in prison under my belt—I was a seasoned employee by then. I told him that his teacher would have to come ask me herself.

About 30 minutes later, Mrs. Parker came over and asked to borrow a keyboard so she could see for herself what her students were marveling over. A couple of them noticed the keyboards in my room and went to ask her to order a few for her high school program. I graciously handed her a keyboard and book thinking it would be returned the same day. Instead, I went completely dark and forgot I lent it out. Because it was a teacher asking, I didn't make a note.

My students were polite enough to allow Mrs. Parker to leave the room before letting me have it non-stop. They amused themselves by ribbing me until the end of the day. All I could do was smile and say, "I'm sorry!" over and over again. They were happy to be cleared of any wrong doings. And, I was happy they graciously accepted my apologies. Otherwise, working with them would not have been any more fun! Word spread that I was the teacher who would not take any stuff. Without realizing it, I was building "prison cred" (as opposed to street cred), and my reputation had spread. As time went on, students knew all about me before entering my class. Maybe it was a good thing after all.

Heart Lesson ~ A rush to judge never makes my heart feel good. I do not have to concern myself with "getting" even with anyone else. I bless each one and move forward with my life.

White building with grey door was back door to my one of the classrooms I taught in during the many years at Folsom. Geese would fly in to enjoy the pond and provide extemporaneous science and nature lessons. This lower yard area was primarily vocational programs and education administrative offices.

CHAPTER 12

Am I Coming Or Am I Going?

There are three types of people in this world. Firstly, there are people who make things happen. Then there are people who watch things happen. Lastly, there are people who ask, what happened? --Steve Backley

During the years as GED teacher, the only thing that topped the first thirty (30) minutes of any day was the thirty minutes in the middle of the day. Both segments were considered prep-time by the administrators and exhale-time by the teachers. The tail end of the day did not count because I was usually comatose by then.

During prep times a number of tasks had to be performed to prepare for the incoming classes: each teacher had two classes of twenty-seven students each—one group in the morning and one in the afternoon. This was a way to stretch the 27 to 1 teacher to student ratio. Then one day, I think someone challenged the supervisors to come up with a way to increase the number of students enrolled and to be sure the teachers did not have time for anything that may have resembled a break.

Without constructing new facilities, there were a finite number of classrooms in the prison. Numbers were the ultimate game. Sitting in the trenches looking up, it felt like the powers that be would have loved to have each teacher work Monday to Saturday, 6 a.m. to 6 p.m. with an auditorium full of students. I thank the Universe for Unions! At the State level of bureaucracy, unions were like lion tamers. The lions being administrators, managers, and supervisors, or the tin man, scare crow, and lion sometimes all wrapped into one.

There were those who had no brains. There were those who had no real courage, and those who had no hearts. The ones with the hearts did not last long. They were rooted out like weeds and given healthy doses of herbicides. The brainless were promoted often based on the illusion of courage. Therefore, dumb ideas ran rampant! The concept of teamwork was divided into "them" versus "us" plan.

Unions were certainly the necessary force and buffer from dumb ideas. However, many dumb ideas slipped through to simply prove how idiotic they actually were. With teachers being the front line workers in this game, they were sometimes forced to allow the silliness to run its course. Imagine my surprise when I learned that the teacher contract did not specify the 'frequency' of the 27 to 1, student-teacher ratio! On short notice, the upper level teachers were informed that the number of classes would increase from two classes of 27 per day for the week, to five classes of 27 per week with each class meeting twice a week. Just trying to explain this can be confusing so please follow along.

Classes would be labeled A,B,C,D, and E. The A class would meet Monday morning from 7 to 10:30 a.m. and again on Wednesday afternoon from 11:30 a.m to 3 p.m. The B class would convene at 11:30 a.m. to 3 p.m. on Mondays and would meet again Thursday morning from 7 am to 10:30 a.m. The C class would begin Tuesday mornings and again on Thursday afternoon. The D class got their start for the week on Tuesday afternoon, and met again on Friday mornings. Finally, E class would begin their school week on Wednesday mornings, and meet again on Friday afternoons. This would allow the teachers to see 27 students times 5 classes or 135 students per week.

Since illogical ideas are not easy to explain, this may be challenging. The logistics of moving prisoners within the institution to accommodate this schedule was a nightmare because education was not the only program operating. There were all kinds of work details all over that were vital to the prison, many having to do with culinary, maintenance, and library. Yes, the library because of all legal work going on as required by law. This schedule was going to cause numerous problems for other staff and prisoners. When there is a problem caused by Education, teachers caught grief and things that would normally be easy to achieve, often turned into tangled messes.

It took days for the Institutional Assignment Office to get all students selected and placed in classes for school. By the time this schedule was implemented, I discovered that many students had been mis-assigned as they already had GEDs or high school diplomas, many students were about to transfer or parole, many stayed locked in their cells and could not get out, many had passes to report to other places, many were confused because they were working on jobs they enjoyed, and there were a select few who just refused. I won't even discuss the routine for getting a student un-assigned once they have been placed in class. Teachers were required to account for each student during their school day.

Keep in mind that learning is supposed to be happening in this brief 3.5 hour span of class time. By the time I finished attendance and tracking a student's absence, class time was either over or down to the last 30 minutes. New students had to get my orientation which was one-on-one with me, sign the institutional and classroom rules, new folders set up, overview of class routine and a discussion of their educational goals and safety rules. With an open entry, open exit policy, students could be placed in classes or removed from classes at will and this happened regularly. By the time I was able to get to the board to teach angles, triangles, Pythagorean Theorem, and essay writing, it was time to dismiss class. Yes, I laughed often and right out loud to keep from going crazy!

Somewhere in the madness, it was expected that I do testing to be sure the student was appropriately placed, and maintain all records. I had two teacher clerks who, because of educational policy, were not allowed to touch student files or testing booklets. The test itself took at least six hours to administer and not all students needed to test. The testing students were often required to cope with ongoing noise in the room as others were working on lessons with neighbors because this teacher was 'tied and bound' by someone's dumb idea.

There were other details that had to be addressed during a class session such as sick students, phone calls—incoming and outgoing, unexpected copies, ordering supplies, and anything else that could not get done during the 30 minute prep time. Something as simple as managing supplies for 135 students was challenging because: 1) supervisors did not want clerks to handle supplies (yet, the reason why all teachers had clerks was to help lighten the mundane load); 2) most times I had to explain why I needed so many pencils and so much paper (if you didn't work with 135+ students per week I guess you would not grasp this dilemma—and I had no time to be the pencil cop); 3) the budget, the budget, the budget (blaming the budget was a constant fail safe for supervisors, but it never worked because school had to go on).

In GED, my classroom was in a trailer on the opposite side of the prison yard from Main Education where supplies were kept. Therefore, in order to get white board cleaner, I had to take my empty spray bottle over to the Main Building for a refill. Once refilled, I had to be sure to keep it in a locked cabinet so those students fighting addictions would not pilfer it away for drinking later. In fact all supplies had to be locked as anything could eventually be used as weapon stock, tattoo ink, or sold on the yard by some entrepreneurial soul.

It got so ridiculous that one day an officer said, "You should not give prisoners pens!" Never mind that we had been using pens in correctional education for decades because students had to write their GED essays in INK. But rather than explain this, I spun around and said, "When you stop giving them razors, I'll stop giving them pens!" What could he say? There was already a mind boggling number of ways to interfere with teaching and learning, I did not want to hear about one more that day.

The five-class nightmare fizzled out in less than three months. It felt great to get back to the two classes a day where I could memorize all 54 names and recognize the faces. And, it felt great to get back to more teaching and a lot less paperwork. Two classes were a challenge, but it was a challenge that one teacher could stay on top of without going insane.

Regardless of all the dumb, idiotic, and downright stupid rules, policies, and procedures, I always enjoyed working with the students. My best days were when I could close the door to the prison world and enter my classroom to be a teacher. Based on all of the positive feedback, my students felt the same way. When learning was happening we were all in a happy zone and earning GEDs.

I had a GED All Star wall with a picture of two men jumping to put the ball in the hoop thanks to my clerk at the time who was a fantastic artist. Upon successful completion of the GED, a student would be transferred to a new program. But, before leaving, he could retire his 'jersey'. The jerseys, in the color of construction paper they chose, measured approximately 6 by 8 inches printed with name and GED date. This simple motivational tool became the envy of the school, and I had students from other classes wanting a jersey on the wall too. But, this small space was reserved for my students who were willing and working to beat the odds!

Heart Lesson ~ It always works best when I work to do my best in any situation. This feels better than being critical and cynical; these are weapons of fear.

CHAPTER 13

A Little Rumble In The Big Pen

The only disability in life is a bad attitude!
--Gregg Braden

Squeezed into our two, 30-minute prep times were record keeping, photocopying as needed, cleaning of the classroom, materials in place, restroom breaks, errands/inter-departmental phone calls, teacher meals, and possibly student counseling just to name a few things.

One beautiful sunny day found me in the middle of trying to exhale after an exhausting three hours with the first class of the day. Adult prisoners in a classroom can be bigger energy drainers than kindergarteners, especially if those adults want to act like five year olds. I substituted in a kindergarten class once, many years ago, and it was enough to make me decide to stay away from elementary school.

As the students were leaving class, a wave of relief swept over me. Just as the last two students were leaving, I noticed the same two students backing into the room while staring at something outside in the break area. Then three more students were backing up into the room staring in the same direction. It snapped my breath to a halt as I instinctively knew that whatever grabbed their undivided attention outside was calling for my immediate action.

I dashed to the door in a matter of seconds to see two students rolling in the dirt with fists pounding away on each other. Both were over six feet tall—one was over 300 pounds and the other was slightly less than 200 pounds. I was witnessing a very interesting situation. The larger of the students was on top and he his face was covered in a rusty orange liquid that had combined with saliva and sweat. There were two correctional officers on their knees attempting to reach through the chain link, razor wired fence to separate the combatants. One of the officers had emptied his pepper spray directly in to one combatant's face from the other side of the fence.

Questions sprang to mind: how long had this been going on? Where is the education officer? Where was the armed guard in the tower that overlooked the entire area? Why hadn't the officers reaching through the fence called out? There was no time for more questions and no time for answers! I pushed the button on my personal alarm. I yelled for everyone on the break yard and in the classroom to get down. All students knew exactly what to do when an alarm was sounded, but the entertainment factor was so intense, they forgot.

The students seated in the break area were paying attention to every little detail that was occurring as if they were human video recorders. This was so they would know exactly what to conveniently forget. Prison rats have their own battles with which to contend. For most, it's far easier to just forget when questioned by the custody officers, but have instant and total recall when reliving the story for their yard buddies and cellmates.

Within a couple of minutes, officers were swarming the break area and separating the fighters. The combatants looked relieved—neither one appeared to be winning, nor did they want to keep fighting. Both men were exhausted and covered in pepper spray. They wanted it to end, but didn't have the courage to break it off on their own. The fight had to be stopped by an outside force so neither would appear to be defeated. They grumbled under their breath as they were being cuffed and escorted to the holding cages where they waited to be questioned. After questioning, both were taken to Administrative segregation to wait completion of the investigation.

Once the area was cleared, the rest of the students were released from education. I had to write an incident report that was submitted as part of the investigation and for the record. Approximately two days later, those two students showed up on a list as 'removed' from their assignment and two new students showed up for school. This partially explains why it's necessary to have 'open entry/open exit' classes. You never know when students will be leaving for a variety of reasons or when they will be enrolled to fill a vacancy.

I learned that two months later, one of the fighters paroled, and the other came to my classroom to beg for his seat back. This was one time that I was glad student assignments were not under my control. My only response was, "The class is full and there are no vacancies. You will have to go to the assignment office." I'm not sure what kind of medication this student was on, but he was definitely delusional. On the one hand, his mind needed to focus on the structured work. On the other hand, school was fertile ground for playing psych games with others. His non-stop teasing of the other students is what started the fight, and his attitude was going to keep him in trouble. The games he enjoyed were a way to break up the monotony in his days.

In 21 years, the only other time I had a fight in my classroom was when one student tossed a balled up piece of paper on another student's desk as he was passing. I had just stepped into the hallway to counsel a student when I heard yelling and loud noises. I turned to look in the window to see a sea of desks being pushed towards the back of the room. There was literally no walking room in the classroom.

This was a computer room with 12 computers on desks around the outer walls of the room and tables and chairs in the center of the room to seat another 12 students who were always waiting to use a computer. If I ever wanted to get to the back of this small room, I had to announce, "Suck it in, I'm heading to the back." Each chair was in direct contact with a chair behind it. This was a problem waiting to happen.

Even with the alarm sounding, the two combatants were too busy trying to get their point across with their fists to stop. The Education Officer was around the corner and at my door in seconds. He immediately saw the fight and dove into the fray. The others in the class were busy trying to make room for the fight. No one dared to break up the fight for fear of getting hurt or mistaken as one of the instigators. The officer grabbed each man by the collar and dragged both out of the room together. It was a bit amusing to watch them dance to keep up with him. The yard officers were already entering the front of the building to take it from there.

The students were taken to the lock-up cages and interrogated immediately. I know because the Captain was on the phone calling me before I could get back to my classroom. I was surprised as he explained that both students admitted they were horse playing and were very sorry to disrupt the class. Both wanted to extend a personal apology and promised to behave if permitted to come back to school. Larry and Curly were back the next day on their very best behavior.

After all is said and done, I am thrilled that nothing ever got too out of hand or too serious in my classes. Most of the time, students preferred to be in class as opposed to sitting in their cells going stir crazy. I am grateful that the circumstances of life made working with prisoner students the easiest part of my day. I only have to reflect on Columbine, Sandy Hood, and the many other public school shootings to realize that the prison classroom was a safer zone. What a backward and confusing world we live in during this era.

Heart Lesson ~ I always enjoy more blessings than I can count. I live with a grateful, loving heart.

Vocational Janitorial Classroom

CHAPTER 14

Mad Dog

Don't believe what your eyes are telling you.
All they show is limitation. Look with your
understanding, find out what you already know,
and you'll see the way to fly. —Richard Bach

Staff restrooms in some areas of the prison seem just as ancient as the prison itself. There were plenty of worksites where men and women had to share the same little comfort station. This caused one to have to do a little extra cleaning or sanitizing before using the facilities. At the end of the day, it was always the porter's job to clean, mop, and refresh the paper supplies.

On one occasion when I entered the restroom, I noticed someone had taped a note to the tank lid that read: It's bad enough that your aim is bad and you pee on the floor, but if you pee on the seat, please have the decency to clean up behind your nasty self.

I knew that note was going to irritate the heck out of someone. There are many who work in prison that do not need to be there because it's too easy to push their buttons. We all have known people who enjoy pushing buttons just for the reactions—they are frustrated individuals. For those who love to push other people's buttons, there are plenty of opportunities. And, as this note demonstrated, someone found an opportunity to create a button pushing contest. I got a good chuckle and didn't think any more of the matter.

Before too long, someone entered the little office I shared with my teaching partner in the back of our classroom and asked if I taped the note to the toilet. Of course, it wasn't me and I had no idea who did it. But, this individual tried to prove a case for me being the culprit. It never feels good to be accused of something you didn't do. Something about the way I looked or the way I worked made me look guilty. I don't know why the accusatory finger was pointing at me, but I let them know that with 60 students, I had no time to write notes. When I laughed over this ridiculous comedy, I must have appeared to be guilty which made me laugh harder. Later that day, they found the note writer who defended her position. The restroom was cleaned and life went on.

While I was out on medical leave following the stroke, my teaching partner called everyday to check on my progress and to keep me apprised of the activities at work. He was now working solo with 60 students. One day he mentioned that there was a new member in the Lifer's Forum. This was a group of life-term prisoners who individually shared their stories with the men who were about to be released. Their talks fell under the umbrella of "This Could Be You." In other words, if anyone in class felt they had the opportunity to parole from prison and do anything to endanger their parole status; their return to prison could be with a life sentence. Collectively, their messages made a powerful, eye-opening statement.

Mad Dog was the newest member to join the Lifer's Forum. Almost every phone call to me in the hospital included an update on how great Mad Dog was and how responsive the students were to his presentation. Naturally, I couldn't wait to meet him and to hear his story. One day during my first week back, Mad Dog was scheduled to talk to the class. I was at my desk in the little office when Mad Dog arrived. One of the clerks signaled to let me know he was here. I went to the counter that divided the office from the classroom to shake his hand. I extended my hand, gave him a firm shake using both of my hands to clasp his hand and told him that I had heard so much about him that I couldn't wait to meet him.

He shook my hand, and his deep blue eyes were serious. He commented that he had heard a lot about me too. I went on to thank him for being courageous enough to fill the position and to talk to our room full of students. After all, most people fear public speaking. He mentioned that he didn't know he had what it took to do it until he tried. And so far, he was enjoying the experience.

The thing about Mad Dog was his appearance. He was in his early 40's and bald. He sported a detailed dragon tattoo that began on one cheek, curled around the back of his head with the dragon tail curling around to the other cheek. There were cartoon characters added here and there including one that resembled the cartoon character, Woody Woodpecker, on his forehead.

I was thankful that it was mandatory for all students in education to wear chambray shirts and blue jeans. This kept all other tattoos out of my sight. While interesting, judging these artful displays was not my business. There was a time I did ask as the student had a phone number tattooed on his upper back between his neck and shoulder. He said his father did that when he was a child. His father felt the streets were so violent that he would one day lose his son to this madness. With the phone number branded on, authorities would know who to call.

It was now time for Mad Dog to address the class. I asked him if he wanted me to introduce him or if he wanted to introduce himself. With a curious look in his eye, he started walking to the front of the room and said he'd take care of it. Once in front, he paced back and forth for a couple of minutes while shaking his head. Then he finally stopped, turned to the class, and said, "I'm just trying to get myself together because that lady in the back, Ms. Carter, just blew my mind!" He went on to explain how no one had ever given him such a warm reception before. He always figured that his tattoos scared people away and most couldn't get beyond the sight of him. But, "Ms. Carter treated me as if she couldn't see any of these tattoos. That shook me for a moment. That lady's something else."

What Mad Dog didn't understand was that neither his tattoos nor anyone else's tattoos meant anything to me. Prison administrators don't want to know this because "Gang Updates" were a regular part of our annual training. I know it's important to them, but for me, I had to work with students and other prisoners regardless of what they looked like, regardless of gang connections, nationality, religious affiliations, or any other identifying factors. Education and learning over rode all of those things to keep me on a level playing field in the prison environment. If I stopped at his tattoos, I would not have gotten to know the real him.

I've long forgotten Mad Dog's real name, but I will always remember the lessons he taught the class that day in his own unique way. Being a member of the human race who happens to have brown skin, I am often judged before people get to know the real me. It may be the nature of our world, but if something different is to be, it has to begin with me. I trust that when Mad Dog paroled, he went on to live that very lesson. In that way, he will continue to be the teacher of how fear blinds and builds barricades, but compassion heals and builds bridges.

Heart Lesson: I feel safer and more at home with myself when I show love and compassion toward others. Showing disdain or hatred leaves me feeling distressed.

CHAPTER 15

Isolation

*Power is of two kinds. One is obtained by the fear of
punishment and the other by acts of love. Power based on love
is a thousand times more effective and permanent then the one
derived from fear of punishment. --Mahatma Gandhi*

Isolation! One would think that being in prison away from society
was isolation. However, when a prisoner's behavior demands more,
CDC certainly has more! Isolation in prison is achieved in a unit called
Administrative Segregation (Ad. Seg.). Ad. Seg. in older times was
known as "The Hole." In Ad. Seg. Prisoners are only out of their cells
for one hour a day and often that one hour is spent in a human kennel
cage—for lack of a better term.

For more extended periods of time, some prisons have Segregated
Housing Units (SHU). A term in SHU is as restricted as it gets. Personal
property is limited—no TV, no radio, no phone calls. Any visit takes
place behind a glass window. So, a solitary existence prevails for a
determined amount of time—sometimes years. SHU is the highest level
of maximum security that the state has developed. They are the notorious
cell blocks located only in a few designated prisons throughout the state.
The most infamous and high powered prisoners are sent there to live out
an indeterminate term. SHU is a prison with in a prison. Eventually,
those deemed worthy are returned to the general prison population.

It was hard for me to imagine, but I had a student assigned to class one day who had spent ten consecutive years in a SHU program. I didn't even want to know what Mr. Jones' problem was—I just figured it was something too complicated for me. All I knew was that I planned on showing him the same level of respect and attention that I gave to all my other students.

Mr. Jones was quiet, reserved, and apprehensive. He asked if he could pull his desk to a corner and sit away from the rest of the students. People and noise bothered him. As the room contained 27 students and was only so big, there was no escape. So, I let him move his desk a couple of feet. He was happy that I did not argue the issue.

I had just divided the class into five groups of five with a couple extra here and there. Each group had to prepare a different lesson on fractions, come up with problems to demonstrate on the board, and problems the class could work on together. This strategy worked well with adult learners as it caused them to focus and learn what they were going to teach. They had to be able to answer questions from the other students. Most were cooperative and respectful because they knew they were going to have a turn in the front of the class too.

It didn't take long for Mr. Jones to seek me out to let me know he didn't work well in groups. He said he preferred to do any assignment I gave him alone. I encouraged him to try to make it work. In fact, we had a discussion about how important it was to learn to work with others. When he sensed that I was not going to budge, he asked to see the psych.

When a student makes that request in prison, it is understood that the teacher will respond as soon as it is logistically feasible. I called the psych office and notified them that Mr. Jones needed to speak with someone right away. There were three prior instances where he had the same request. I really had to handle this fragile being with care. I didn't want any psychotic breakdowns in my class. He left class and was in the psych department in short order. And, he was back in my class before I had time to miss him.

Without having to be asked he said, "The psych told me that group work would be good for me and I should try!" After his pronouncement, he went back to his group and began trying to help his group with the assignment. I had never witnessed such obedience. The "psych" must have had a powerful "psych" going.

It was a relief to know I was on the right track and that Mr. Jones was being cooperative about the whole thing. I made it a point to compliment his behavior before the end of the day, and he smiled. He was on the path to re-integration. He engaged in all other assignments with an eagerness to learn and to do a good job. Mr. Jones settled into a comfortable learning mode until he transferred to another prison the following year. I trust he left in a better position to make new adjustments.

Heart Lesson ~ Instead of focusing on all that I perceive to be unfair in this world, I focus on all of the good that is always around me.

Cell Block B—one of the first at Folsom from 1880.
Still open for business as of this publishing.

Many enjoyed the solitude. Others felt claustrophobic.

CHAPTER 16

A Cross To Bear

For, what other dungeon is so dark as one's own heart!
What jailer so inexorable as one's self!
--Nathaniel Hawthorne

As a Re-Entry teacher, one of my favorite workshops was the one on parenting. Color me crazy, but I always felt that in working with my select group of students, it was always best to "cut to the chase" and get right to the heart of things. My guess would be that any class I ever had in prison was comprised of at least 75 percent parents—married or otherwise. As a parent, we all typically discipline our children they way our parents disciplined us. Those who got spanked, and we remember the spankings and remember if those spankings were effective.

I did not need research to prove this as I had first-hand knowledge. My introduction to school was at a parochial elementary school in New Jersey. There, teachers included corporal punishment as part of the curriculum. In fact, spankings with a belt and smacks with the paddle were typically addressed in the mornings right after our prayers and pledge of allegiance to the flag but before mathematics. The boys were required to take off their belts and lay across the teacher's, habit draped lap for spankings to the behind. The girls had to stand with their hands out, palms up to be smacked with the thick ruler. Due to our mandatory uniforms of skirts and blouses, it would have been inappropriate for girls to lie across someone's lap.

If anyone catches me acting a tad strange, I can point the finger at the order of nuns who felt that I was being defiant because I learned to write with my left-hand, or because I was sitting instead of kneeling in mass. Yes, it was in Latin. Even at five years old, having to hold my hands out for the ruler to whack me never made sense. I *always,* out of instinct, pulled my hands back. This stunt earned me double whacks and a second nun to hold my hands in place! The teacher would lay the pencil on my desk and ask me to write my ABCs. I naturally picked up the pencil with my left-hand. Without an explanation to my understanding, I felt that I was being punished for no earthly good reason. After three years of this torture without success, my parents switched me over to public school. Thank Heavens!

It was sometime in adulthood that I was able to connect the dots after learning that there was an era when Catholics viewed anything not on the right-hand side of God as evil and sinister. As far as this Order of nuns was concerned, I obviously was full of the devil. I considered it a feat to continue to be left-handed. To my detriment, however, there may have been a loss as I became so hard headed and strong willed that I became a difficult child and did not like myself.

I learned that hitting others was how to solve problems, and sometimes it was fun to hit for no good reason. This behavior did not go over well with my younger brothers or my parents. My brothers started hitting back and my parents would intercede with spankings. We were all playing a part in creating a cycle of violence. I somehow knew I had to change my behavior.

As a teacher and a parent, my common sense dictated that hitting never solved anything. And, when you want to teach someone not to hit, you do not hit to make the point! Of course, I have the same feeling about capital punishment. We as a State or a Nation, kill people to teach them that killing is not the way to go. If either capital punishment or spanking worked, there would be no need for it centuries later. Resorting to violence says that we are at the ends of our limits for thinking and patience. If we call ourselves a civilized nation, is that really what civilized people do? Or, do we call ourselves a civilized nation just so we can teach what an oxymoron is?

When spanked, many children heard the words: "I'm doing this because I love you," and "This is going to hurt me more than it hurts you." And, they grew up believing this bologna. These words will never make sense to any thinking person. I encouraged my students to think and reminded them that Love doesn't hurt, and if it hurts, it's not love (A Course In Miracles). We have to learn to separate those ideas. Once we stop confusing things, life becomes less complicated. The little ones look to the adults for answers that will help make this big world understandable. Yet, we cannot teach what we do not know.

My purpose in presenting this information was to encourage alternatives to violence and to motivate students to always keep an open mind to allow new information to enter. If they found it useful, good—if not, they could toss it out and nothing was lost. Parenting and no spanking was such a meaty issue to present and discuss that I brought in a gentleman from the Bay Area of California who operated a non-profit organization called "Project No Spank." He was a retired teacher and had been instrumental in getting spanking removed from many school districts. Yes, public schools used to spank children on a regular basis.

By way of introducing the guest speaker, I would walk to the board and draw a giant cross. Then, I would turn to the class and ask, what is this? They all shouted out, "A Cross." I said, "That's right. Before today's presentation is over, you are going to want to crucify me, so I brought my own cross. I would face them, and stretch my arms out to fit the cross on the board. This always got their attention, and so began the lesson.

There was too much researched information to present to the class or in this story. But, the things that stood out most to me, was the whole idea that spanking on the backside, where the spine ends and vital nerves travel down the legs can be physically damaging to a child and traumatizing to the body thereby creating other problems. There's even research that shows spanking can cause gender confusion. Every time we strike out to hit a child, it is a pronouncement that we have reached the end of ability to think clearly. As adults, we should always be able to think of ways to get the message across to children in nonviolent yet understandable ways.

For example, my son loved to play with his toys all over the house and leave them for me to pick up. One day when he was three years old, we had a talk. I let him know that I buy the things he likes to play with so he can have fun. If he leaves them on the floor, it means he does not like them anymore. If he liked them, he would put them back in his room in the toy chest. So, from now on, if mommy finds a toy on the floor, she is going to throw it away for him in the trash can.

The very next day I noticed my son going through the trash can to be sure none of his things were there. He found his teddy bear. On the second day, he found a couple of his MatchBox cars. By day three, the lesson was fully incorporated into his little world and all toys were back in place by the end of the day. This was certainly far easier and less stressful on everyone than spanking and yelling.

Not all, but many of my students throughout the years never took time to understand what it meant to be a parent. I always hoped that this workshop would break cycles of violence in their households so they could begin to make a difference. Yet, the push-back I got from many left me wondering. After presenting a day full of information, guest speaker, and videos, many still wanted to justify their right and determination to spank. The good news was, in a day or two after the information had been digested, a few students would say, "Thank You!" I'm beginning to see spanking in a different light, and the message makes more sense now.

Heart Lesson ~ When I see the unwillingness in others to change their minds, let me be sure I am willing to change my mind especially when the change can benefit me.

A one man cell converted for two men when system is overcrowded. Cells are searched on a routine basis.

CHAPTER 17

Bred To Hate

A child weaned on poison considers harm a comfort.
--Gillian Flynn

The practice of discrimination is highlighted upfront to put this story in context. First of all, why does any correctional facility perpetuate and condone racism on a whole scale level? Whenever I had to cross that infamous Folsom Prison yard to get to the Main Education Building, I could clearly see different groups congregating in different areas of the yard. This practice was allowed to go on the entire length of my employment. It existed before I arrived and I'm pretty certain, it continued after I left.

Different gang members claimed their section of the yard and others could not stop without cause in those areas. The prisoners were not allowed to be housed together even if it was their request; a practice enforced by the prison. This broad practice fell under the umbrella of health, safety, and control. But, I always appreciate when someone who is tired of the status quo, decides to challenge illegal/ questionable practices. Why are we doing this? There has to be a better way.

For years, this policy was allowed to exist until a prisoner filed a law suit to have this discrimination policy changed. The following is from an article published online by RT©Autonomous Non-Profit Organization on April 13, 2013.

> *Though correctional officials with the State of California deny racial targeting, some inmates have come forward with complaints, and in 2011 filed a class action lawsuit claiming racial discrimination.*
>
> *Robert Mitchell, an inmate at High Desert State Prison, testified that he had been swept up into recurring lockdowns because he is black, and had suffered muscular atrophy and pain as he was prevented from exercising a leg injury.*

The article goes on to highlight the fact that the Supreme Court ruled that "When government officials are permitted to use race as a proxy for gang membership and violence…society as a whole suffers."

And, the following is an excerpt from an article published by Christine Thompson in PRO PUBLICA ON APRIL 12, 2013:

> *In several men's prisons across California, colored signs hang above cell doors: blue for black inmates, white for white, red, green or pink for Hispanic, yellow for everyone else.*
>
> *Though it's not an official policy, at least five California state prisons have a color-coding system.*
>
> *State and federal courts have ruled against the practice multiple times. One state court judge concluded in 2002 that "managing inmates on the basis of ethnicity" was counterproductive, and instead increased hostilities among prisoners.*

Unfortunately, prisons work hard to justify the need to discriminate on this level without being concerned about the deleterious effects it has on the very individuals they are working to rehabilitate, or the impact on the staff members who have to enforce these racial practices.

These two excerpts are included so you will know this is not a personal conspiracy theory. Even with these non-discrimination laws, it has taken years to make it a workable policy because of the historical lines etched in the minds of staff and prisoners. If discriminatory practices exist in the prison with prisoners, what keeps some from employing those practices with staff? I think it is easy to conclude that in many instances, there is no distinction. So, this has to be a concern for everyone.

I realize you may call this control in an environment where control is necessary. However, this practice is more harmful than anyone realizes. If nothing else, consider the fact that the majority of these men will be going home one day. They will take with them much of what was learned in prison. If they learn to perpetuate racism and hate through a variety of discriminatory practices, this is what goes home. Ultimately, racist attitudes keep you personally imprisoned and "you" wind up becoming your own worst enemy. As the world is trying to move forward in these areas, our prisons must also move forward.

Chris was a young man in his early twenties. I mention age because he seemed to be wise beyond his years. Then again, prison has a way of catching you up and pushing you up to the plate of maturity. If you are willing to learn from your experiences, you wise-up rapidly.

One of the outside volunteers who came every month to the Pre-Release Program always had a powerful message about being the man you were meant to be. At the end of his talk, he would request that all student desks be pushed against the wall so there was plenty of floor space for everyone to sit in a circle. Each man was asked to share what he learned while doing his time and what he looked forward to once he paroled. Little did they know what a powerful opportunity this would be to learn from others. It was a time for truth and honesty.

During this particular circle time, I want to point out that Chris was sitting mid-way in the circle. He got to hear approximately 30 others who came before him. He was small in stature but when it was his turn to talk; his words were those of a giant! He didn't cower or mumble. He put his honesty before this group of men and his words captured everyone.

Chris explained that it was nice to hear all the other guys talk about looking forward to going home and being with their loved ones and friends. Others had mentioned the family support that was waiting for them and how that would help them ease their way back into society.

He said that he wished he could look forward to the same kinds of things. But, his family "bred him to hate" and to be a racist—he couldn't go back.

With tears gently rolling down his face, Chris spoke about what he witnessed in prison that taught him they were all the same, with the same problems and challenges in life. In their sameness, the color of one's skin did not matter as all colors were incarcerated. He had gotten to work with men of different ethnicities and once he got to know them, there was no fear and no hate. They were all dealing with the same prison issues and problems in much the same way. Sometimes, these are the kinds of life lessons that only experience itself can impart. A teacher explaining how racism is unhealthy would not have been as effective in delivering the message as Chris. In this circle, Chris became the teacher of experience.

As soon as Chris finished, others in the circle were offering him their hand in help. One said he would leave him a name and address for an agency looking to hire. Another gave him an idea on where to find housing. Still another invited him to come home with him because his family would love him. Just about everyone commented that they could feel his honesty and his fear. While the rest of the men finished their turn in the circle, Chris' words stayed uppermost in everyone's mind. We heard the others, but we did not feel their words in the same way.

My mind wanted to know what kind of self-imposed terror Chris faced on his first days in prison. What thoughts ran through his mind when he discovered the very people he had learned to hate and run from were the ones he had to come face-to-face with in prison. I can guess that one thought had to be, this must be HELL. Now, the majority of those offering help that day were once his sworn enemies. All of this was further evidence that it is love of humankind that makes the world go around.

The powerful feeling Chris shared with us is still crystal clear after approximately 12 years. Life often gives us the test before it gives us the lesson! In the midst of the test, many have died. The test for Chris was surviving prison with all ethnicities. He made it to parole, and I would love to know how Chris went on with his life. I can only pray that his family was not waiting for him at the gate upon release. In that way, he would have some sense of hope in leaving all racism behind. I just heard someone say that bigotry is a disease of the mind. If it is a disease, it can be cured with learning and practicing unconditional love for all life regardless of what form that life may look like. This is part of spiritual maturity, and this maturity benefits all of humankind.

Heart Lesson ~ When minds are expanded by new and bigger ideas, it's difficult to go back to old ways of thinking. Our hearts will protest.

CHAPTER 18

Changing Minds

*If a soul is left in the darkness, sins will
be committed. —Victor Hugo*

The Lifer's Forum was a group of life term prisoners who wanted
to share their stories with the Pre-Release class in an effort to make
an impact on those who were about to parole. They operated with the
presentation format of, "This Could Be You." For the men about to
leave prison and move on to happier times, a return to prison was the
last thing on their minds. However, for the many who listened to what
the lifers had to say; I do think it made an indelible impression.

Many of the stories I heard over the five years that I taught this
particular class left a lasting impact on me too. One such story was
of a tall blond-haired, blue-eyed young man who, in his hay-day,
reveled in the manufacture of methamphetamines. He would share
his wild days of running from the sheriffs in and around Southern
California. He had a sense of entitlement over his right to earn a
living any way he wanted. Sam would try to compare himself to the
people of long ago whose financial foundation was built on bootleg
alcohol before they turned legitimate. He saw himself as one of them
who would eventually be on the side of the law as soon as he had
enough money.

After a wild shootout with the sheriff's in the San Diego area, Sam was convicted on several counts and sentenced to life. His stupidity followed him to prison. He found a way to continue his drug activity in prison. As the expression goes, Sam had more games than Milton Bradley. It was a natural extension to continue with the lucrative pattern he knew best.

However, with a life sentence, he had to figure out how to deal with the challenges on the inside. In prison, money comes in many forms, the least of which is cash. Prisoners found with cash can be prosecuted. Money can be sent in to be placed on their account, but they never get to get it in their hands. Other forms of money include: items from the canteen, tobacco, goods sent in from outside vendors, services rendered, i.e., clothes washed and ironed, errands, and anything else a nefarious mind could dream up.

Sam's business was a bit tougher to handle in prison, but that was not enough to stop a man on a mission. There were still plenty of drug habits that needed his attention. One day when he was out in the visiting patio, he saw a prisoner with one of those habits who owed him money. When Sam glanced over at the guy, Sam noticed he was yelling at his girlfriend and giving her a hard time. It seems she didn't have any money to sneak in to him. Sam noticed a young boy standing near the girlfriend. The young one appeared to be about six years old. He had blonde hair and blue eyes just like Sam.

As Sam studied the little fellow, he noticed the little one's dirty clothes, tattered shoes, and unkempt hair. He reminded Sam of himself at that age of innocence—far too young to have to be exposed to prison. At that moment, all sorts of things ran through Sam's head including the pressure he was indirectly imposing on this young lad and his naive mother because of his drug business.

Left: Visiting building and patio. Also where graduations are held. (Previously Education Building prior to 1990s.)

Sam tells the story that this was a turning point for him. He grew disgusted with himself and could no longer stand his own thoughts of what he had been doing. He was finally making the connection of how he had hurt countless other children over the years because of his illicit drug activities. The thoughts that swirled through his head brought tears to his eyes that day.

Hard headed prisoners are an interesting bunch. Sometimes I could see them banging their own heads against the wall. For whatever reason, most continued even when I would try to intervene. One day after talking myself silly to a class of hardheads, I stepped into the hallway, leaned against the wall and shook my head. Just then a young prisoner came around the corner and saw me. He asked, "What's wrong Ms. Carter. Are you alright?" I simply said, "What does it take to get through to these guys?" He responded, "Sometimes, it takes them coming back to prison with a capital L stamped on their file.

Sam, who did have an "L" for life-term stamped on his file, went on to tell the story of how he had to compose himself so he could go over to this prisoner to let him know he didn't ever want anything else from him. Instead, he wanted him to use the money to buy his kid some decent clothes and a haircut. He further stated that he wouldn't sell him another ounce of dope because he wanted him to get sober so he could take care of his son. He reminded him that his child needed him to be a good father. Sam encouraged the guy to get clean and to start paying more attention to those who loved him.

With all of the life term prisoners on Old Folsom's mainline at the time, not many were brave enough to step up to the plate to help others. Many were so resentful of those who had the opportunity to go home; they didn't bother to talk to them. Instead, some of the more disgruntled souls would find ways to sabotage the short termers by enticing them into fights or getting them to break the rules so their sentences could be lengthened. So, for those men who bravely came to be a motivational force for others, I applaud them and offer them encouragement to continue. Their voices are needed. It's more meaningful when one incarcerated soul can uplift and encourage another to do the right thing.

Every time Sam shared that story with the Pre-Release class, he couldn't hold back his own tears. It was painful each time because he kept remembering what his deeds had done to other children. There was always a silence in the class with several heads nodding in understanding. Hopefully, this message helped prisoners get their heads in gear so they could begin to connect the dots in their own lives. Sam reminded everyone that their illegal deeds always had an effect on others even though they might not be able to see those individuals face-to-face. And, if they were willing to forget the valuable message he was sharing, they too would one day be the ones who stood before a class of paroling men to utter the words: "This Could Be You!"

This is yet another reason why I always kept the door to my heart open for people to make meaningful changes in their lives. I was not a believer in once a con, always a con. Where are we without hope? Sam may not ever be found suitable for parole, but he is already a free man in his own heart. Sam and his story belong to all of us if we are willing to examine it. The question for us is where are we in our own hearts? Can we or are we willing to make the changes in our lives to be more positive, productive beings? Have we ruled out hope? Whatever questions his story stirs in you deserves your attention.

Heart Lesson ~ My judgment of others is often all wrong. I choose to see with the eyes of my heart and through the Wisdom of the Infinite.

CHAPTER 19

Day Dreaming

*Daydream, because you can't accomplish what you've
never fully imagined. --Richelle E. Goodrich*

If I had a buck for every time someone scolded me for daydreaming as a child, I'd be living on a tropical island today! From Mom to my teachers, I was slowly and systematically driven from these mind saving breaks and back to the here and now. I always felt that daydreaming saved me from the insanity of being bored in school, in church, or at home. My daydreams always seemed constructive and futuristic. They took me to places where I could strive to be better. Whenever I returned from a daydream, either by force or naturally, I always returned in a state of serenity and happiness. How could such a wonderful and peaceful experience be so bad in the eyes of so many?

Here is a brief description from Wikipedia defining daydreaming:
Daydreaming *is a short-term detachment from one's immediate surroundings, during which a person's contact with reality is blurred and partially substituted by a visionary* <u>fantasy</u>, *especially one of happy, pleasant thoughts, hopes or ambitions, imagined as coming to pass, and experienced while awake. There are many types of daydreams, and there is no consistent definition amongst* <u>psychologists</u>, *however the characteristic that is common to all forms of daydreaming meets the criteria for mild* <u>dissociation</u>.

Naturally, when a student I'll call Mr. B stood transfixed in the corner of the classroom, I was inclined to leave him alone. His stare was always towards the ceiling, and the classroom activity never caught his attention once he was into his daydream. Remembering how much the little girl in me hated to be disturbed during these times, and remembering that Mr. B had been convicted of some kind of felonious crime, I figured I had better leave him alone. His daydreaming absolutely did not bother me one bit and the other students figured he was too crazy to disturb, so it was a happy existence for everyone.

When Mr. B's attention was on class work, he would yell out the correct answers and ask insightful questions. I would often have him go to the board to work on a problem and then explain how he arrived at the answer. Those times brought smiles to his face as he knew he had accomplished something that his fellow classmates were still trying to master. It probably made him feel a bit like the teacher's pet. He enjoyed that position.

While at my desk working, I would look up to find him in the chair for inquiring minds. I called it that so students would not be intimidated to come forward to ask for help for anything even if it was not specifically related to education. I have no doubt that this policy helped squash many a problem and accounts for me having great days at work. Just to get a question answered in prison would often lead to high drama because many got stuck on "why" the question was being asked. Many times the question of "why" was of major concern, because it seemed to signal that some form of manipulation was about to happen. The subject of manipulation is included in many fictional books as it is a delicious base for intrigue.

Mr. B's questions were always related to the fine points of the subject we were discussing. If, for example, the subject were prepositions, he wanted to know how to decide if the word was a preposition or not and how to find the object of the preposition—often that was the next day's lesson. But, if he wanted to move ahead, we moved ahead. Every now and then, he would want to ask a personal question such as,

"How many kids do you have, Ms. C?"

"Are any of them in prison?"

"How can you stand working with these criminals?"

I had to develop a personal policy for answering personal questions. My response was one of three choices: 1) Are you writing a book? If so, leave that chapter out and call it a mystery; 2) Oh, I currently have 27 kids! (That was the number of students in my class.) Or, 3) I'm going to give you a nickel so you can go buy some business of your own and leave mine alone.

Any of these responses would get the message across in a humorous way, don't ask because she's not telling. Besides, they already knew those types of questions were inappropriate. Yet, it did not stop students from asking because they felt any inside information would give them a "leg up" on feeling closer to me and even becoming my friend. I did not go to work in prison to find friends. Therefore, personal pictures or personal conversations in front of students were kept out of the program.

When Mr. B kept getting the same response, he would just smile and know his attempts did not work this time. He'd soon try again—all students did.

Finally, after many months at the 5th to 7th grade level, which was called ABE II (Adult Basic Education), it was time to promote Mr. B to the 8th and 9th grade program, ABE III. I had a fight on my hands because he absolutely did not want to promote. He figured he had found a home in my class and he was as free as a bird to daydream as much as he wanted. It's the nature of the prison environment to keep people and things moving even if it's in a circle or backward. Just keep moving so no one gets comfortable—a security tactic. If prisoners got noticeably comfortable, they were relocated.

After many days, I convinced him it was for his best interest and that he would be alright. Once he left the program, there were 27 other students who demanded my undivided attention, and I soon forgot about Mr. B. Whenever he danced across my mind, I would always smile and send out good wishes for his educational success.

Then one day, as life would have it, I was leaving work and heading toward the prison gate and was walking behind two correctional officers. I could hear their conversation:

"Yeah, by the time we got to him, he was gone."

"The dude used his belt to hang himself."

"He obviously had other issues."

I knew in that instant they were talking about Mr. B. I interrupted and asked if this inmate was Mr. B. They said,

"Yes, that was his name. He had red hair and chubby cheeks. Did you know him?"

I said, "Oh geez, he used to be my student!"

I walked on and didn't hear anything else they may have said. I started second guessing myself: Did I move him too soon? Why didn't I leave him in my class? Was he being threatened? If he were still in my class, maybe he would have come to me for help? I sent up a prayer for Mr. B and kept moving to get out of the gate. On the way home I naturally reflected on him standing in the corner of the room daydreaming. What was he seeing in his dreams? It had to be happier places for him than prison. Or just maybe, he was seeing a future event. Goethe says: "Future events cast backward shadows." I didn't take the time to investigate any of the details of his death. Once again, there would have been too many questions about "why" I wanted or needed to know. I was just happy that he found a modicum of peace while in my classroom, and was hopefully finding peace in the hereafter.

Heart Lesson ~ When I reflect on others who have entered my life, I'm happy when the reflections are good ones. This lets me know that I was more helpful than not!

Housing Unit 2: Path used to get to the Academic Education Building. The end of this building marked the half way point. The maze-like trek to Education could take up to 15 minutes. Plenty of students hollered out to greet me on the way in each morning.

CHAPTER 20

Revenge

*Throughout life people will make you mad, disrespect you
and treat you bad. Let God deal with the things they do, cause
hate in your heart will consume you too.* — *Will Smith*

All of the men in the Life Forum learned to polish their presentations to be truly motivational to the paroling classes. Several stayed with the same presentation throughout the years. However, there was one individual who seemed to have a natural gift of oratory. He was able to perform impromptu and change his talk frequently so it never became old. And, he was able to speak to a variety of different topics depending on the audience. William was a toastmaster's dream.

Bill, as the men called him, was a blessing for the incarcerated men who would probably never have the opportunity to hear a motivational speaker. He also helped those who had fallen out of grace with their families and friends and those who had come to feel disenfranchised from life inside and outside of prison.

For more than ten years, Bill had given three motivational talks each week to different groups of men from AA to NA and of course once or twice for the Pre-Release Program. If someone was not able to keep their appointment, Bill could be called on to fill in on a moment's notice. Even the roughest guy in the bunch had to concede that Bill had a way of touching them and making them think.

One such character was a guy named Outlaw. Bill told me about Outlaw because he just couldn't figure him out. He described Outlaw as a nefarious looking character who sat in the back corner of the room during the AA meetings seemingly lost in his own world. He didn't talk to anyone other than his "boys." He rarely uttered a word. When anything came out of his mouth it was usually a grunt.

With a roving eye and a distrustful scowl, Outlaw gave the impression that he was determined not to let anyone or anything penetrate his sturdy crafted emotional armor. But, Bill knew that appearances could be deceiving. And the very nature of prison demanded that he have some sort of manly protection. Keeping a positive attitude, Bill continued to do what he did best and prayed that those who needed to hear the message would hear it. Then one day, a miracle appeared to happen.

After the formal part of the AA meeting was over, Bill always gave a pep talk as a way to get the guys to open up and share their stories. While he often felt his words fell on deaf ears, he always knew that those who needed to hear the message would somehow get it. On one day after his talk about forgiveness, Outlaw seemed to come to life. Bill explained that forgiving frees us so that we no longer feel like we are carrying a dead mule. He went on to say that for every vengeful, unforgiving thought, that mule would feel like it weighed a pound heavier.

Bill had no idea of the importance of his message until a week later when Outlaw sought him out. As Bill was crossing the yard, he heard someone holler out his name to the top of their lungs. Bill new it was Outlaw doing the shouting, and he could feel that the whole yard was now at attention including the custody officers. Bill froze in his tracks. He couldn't imagine what Outlaw wanted with him. Bill turned around slowly to find a grinning Outlaw standing in front of him without his usual entourage.

"After that talk you did a few nights back about forgiving, I went back to my cell and tore up a list of names I'd been holding onto for years," Outlaw explained.

"What names?" Bill inquired.

"The names of folks who done stuff to me. Folks who snitched on me and some who didn't come to help me when I thought they should. They all hurt me in some way," said Outlaw.

"Wow!" said Bill, "You really tore the list up?"

"Yep, you got me with that talk about the weight I was carrying and that nobody cared about it but me."

"And, how do you feel about not having that list?" Bill asked.

"It feels weird 'cause I thought it was my job to get even with everybody. I'd been holdin' on to that list and looking it over every week for the past twelve years. Without it, I feel like I done put the mule down," Outlaw said with a smile.

Then without warning, Outlaw gave Bill a big hug right there on the main yard in prison in front of hundreds who were out enjoying night yard. The list was gone. In its place was a lighter heart. Outlaw was a changed man now that he had allowed forgiveness to work in his life—forgiveness of others and himself. It had to be the beginning of more good things to come. Prisoners are routinely moved to other prisons or parole to other parts of the state. We don't know how Outlaw fared with the rest of his life, we just have to believe that it improved for him, for those close to him, and for those who were on the list.

Heart Lesson ~ I will discover new ways to have a lighter heart. That means forgiveness must be in the forefront followed by ongoing doses of gratitude.

Main Exercise Yard—Building 1 in background.
Building 1 is largest in the prison.

CHAPTER 21

What's In A Name?

A nickname is the hardest stone that the devil can throw at a man. --~Author unknown, quoted William Hazlitt

Sasquatch was his name and a double life sentence was his game. The handles or nicknames by which some prisoners are known while in prison are enough to make you scratch a bald spot in your head and wonder aloud what the heck they were thinking. Was the handle part of the persona that went with the false face that most seemed to be wearing? Based on my observations, it was. The individual typically strived to emulate the nickname. In that sense, the person felt he was only "keeping it real." And of course, he was fitting in with mainstream prison life.

For Sasquatch, I never knew if his appearance caught up to his nickname, or if his nickname stuck because of his appearance. Sasquatch was about 6'4" and perhaps 40 years old. He wore his thick, wild mane below his shoulders, and it was as unruly and as wild as his mustache and beard. Beneath this appearance, he was gentle—probably to compensate for his intimidating presence. He rarely spoke in class and when he did, it was in polite tones. For some students it was easy to understand from their behavior and attitude why they came to prison. But for Sasquatch, I never knew unless he was wandering around scaring the daylights out of folks just being himself.

One day as he completed an assignment and was turning it in, he was shaking his head. I asked if he had a question. He looked at me and commented, "Double life—they gave me a double life sentence. What do they want me to do Ms. C, die and come back again?"

As this question certainly had nothing to do with the assignment, I was at a loss for words. In a scramble to find an empathetic response, I simply told him, "No, you don't have to die again and come back. But, obviously the system wants you to have plenty of time to think about everything that has gone on in your life—and the court felt that it could take the rest of your natural life to do it."

That response seemed to make sense to him and he returned to his seat with a sigh. He just wanted a moment to be heard. He was quiet for the rest of that class period. I made a note to keep an eye on him as his next thoughts could have leaned in the direction of suicide. But, during the following days, I found him back to his usual cooperative self.

Over the years the curious handles like Psycho, Commando, Creeper, and Rambo so often meant that the individual had displayed those character traits. It would signal ahead of time to either stay away or engage at your own risk. Handles such as New York, Cuba, TJ, and Oakland let you know where that person was from. Other handles like Snake, Ice, Pops, Lefty, Grizzly, and Cadillac are a few of the names that may speak to a highlight in the person's life. The false masks that these men might have been wearing during the commission of their crimes seemed to keep them trapped in time. If they were to ever reveal their true identity no one would recognize them.

On a rare occasion I would see the transformation unfold in my classroom. A man, who once was referred to and well known by his handle, Popsicle, was telling everyone to refer to him by his real name. And, the time when Satan tried to grow his hair back to cover the menacing looking horns he had tattooed on his forehead. To his dismay, he was old enough to witness his receding hairline that still revealed his horns in their full glory. He was one individual who I am sure was going straight to the tattoo removal shop upon release. It was a wonderful thing to witness many coming of age even though it was in prison.

As a teacher, the only time I used a student's handle was to ascertain their given name. Some of the nicknames followed a person to prison from their neighborhoods. I always wondered if Pre-School's handle followed him. Unfortunately, this handle was fitting based on the way he carried himself. He wore braids that each had a direction of their own. He walked around with his thumb in his mouth while his other hand held up his oversized pants. Pre-School always had a disheveled appearance and you could never understand him because he would not remove that thumb unless he was forced to do so. He did not care what others thought or how much they teased him. Everyone found it was easier to give him plenty of space. No one wanted to test the limits of his childish behavior.

Pre-School was never one of my students, but I always saw him around Education and he always spoke to me. If he had ever been promoted to the GED Program, I would have had to roll up my sleeves as he would have required a lot of time and energy. I think I was saved from this dilemma as I know he would have been working on me as hard as I would have tried to work on him. I did not want that contest of wills to be the one that wore me out. He would have presented all the reasons why he couldn't earn a GED, and I would have presented all of the reasons why he could. I was never happy with a draw.

On another occasion as I was walking through one of the buildings, I saw a small man who looked like a little boy who seemed completely out of place in prison. My first thought was, that was nice he was probably coming to visit his father. Then I realized, there are no outside visitors in housing units, and he was wearing blue jeans and a blue shirt. He was a prisoner! When I got to class that morning, I asked, "Who was the very small man in Five Building?"

The answer was, "That's Chucky, and it's best to leave Chucky alone Ms. C."

"Why?" I pressed.

"Because Chucky is not who he is but "what" he is!"

I immediately understood they were referring to the movie, Chucky, about the little child-like demon doll that went around viscously murdering people with a knife.

I simply responded, "Oh," and left that subject alone. I did not want Chucky in my class trying to live up to his name. Sometimes, it doesn't pay to be too curious.

The other teachers seemed to think that I had a way with these students so they did not hesitate to send me the ones they deemed to be problems. And, I always wanted to be the teacher who gave it a try. My great mission as a teacher was to make things easier to understand, and therefore more fun to learn. Students responded to my patience and compassion. For me it worked, but it did take a lot of time, energy, and dedication.

Heart Lesson ~ Perhaps those who crave freedom are the hungriest for simple kindnesses. There's never a good enough reason to be unkind.

CHAPTER 22

A Homicide at Home

People say walking on water is a miracle. But to me,
walking peacefully on earth is the real miracle.
--Thich Nhat Hanh

When life seems to get tough, I remember that we are but travelers on this earth. We didn't come to stay—we will all pass. So, I work to keep things in perspective and remind myself of the importance to spend our precious moments in love, gratitude, joy, and laughter. For most, maturity brings about this understanding and the sense that what we give to life determines the kind of life we experience. I prefer to be about the business of doing good where I can for others and for our planet. It's simple, but then I have chosen to enjoy a simple life. We can look around and see others who are doing the same in varying degrees. Then, we can look around and see some who appear to live in varying degrees of hate and fear.

After one long ten hour day, I could hear the phone ringing as I entered the door. I dropped my school bag to pick up the phone. It was my brother calling to say that our middle brother, at the ripe old age of 42, had been shot and was presumed dead. I needed to exhale from the day, but did not have the chance as I tried to wrap my mind around the details that were now flying at me: he was at home, someone was there with a gun; he stumbled to the front door and fell outside; he lived long enough to identify his assailant; his son was there to witness the whole thing; he was rushed to the hospital; there was no further information.

From the numbness of my mind, our life as kids flashed before me. We had parents whose purpose was to be sure we had a great childhood. They were not rich in material assets, but they were rich with love. Now, as adults, we were working to do the same for our children. My brother, whom I had grown to love even more in adulthood, was no longer with us. My thoughts immediately centered on my nephew and his well being. As the oldest, I laid out a plan to get more information from the hospital while my younger brother tried to reach family.

Once we learned that our brother had, in fact died, we took care of all arrangements for a funeral in Los Angeles and burial in Sacramento. Due to logistics, it was a two week period from beginning to end. I was grateful for all of the support from family, friends, and colleagues. Three car loads of teachers from the prison came to the cemetery for the graveside service. This turned out to be the lift I didn't even know I needed. I will forever be grateful to each of them.

Finally, the time arrived to report back the prison and to prepare for working with raw emotions and feelings while dealing with my students. Many different thoughts ran through my head. I was teaching people who had come to prison for murder and now my brother had become a murder victim. The time was at hand to see if I could walk my talk and resume a teacher–student relationship without any negative overflow.

When my class reported that morning, I got plenty of stares. Everyone was unusually quiet and very polite. They all indicated they were happy to see me back as they had missed me. There was a substitute, and they all took delight in telling me how that person was no match for me. I did not know what the students were told, but they seemed to know that my brother had died. Yet, I did not know if they knew how he died.

After everyone was in and accounted for, one student who had been designated the ambassador for the class, came and sat in the chair by my desk. He handed me a file folder. I opened it and inside was a homemade sympathy card the class had made for me. There was a beautiful colored rose on the front and a verse inside with signatures from everyone in the class. I was touched and so appreciative that I was at a loss for words. They had obtained permission from the principal to give it to me. As I admired the card, they all expressed their sympathy--their compassion spilled out. What a class!

My students wanted to embrace me like family and share in my grief. They were trying to let me know that everything was going to be all right. They were even trying to apologize for my brother's death as a way of trying to comfort me. It was then I realized I had to let them know how I viewed death and to talk briefly about the grieving process. So, we spent the next hour talking about passing from this physical life and the only place we know.

Many of them had experienced the loss of a loved one while in prison, and they felt helpless because they could not be there for their families. And, all of us are heading for the great "hereafter" experience ourselves. So, perhaps we'd all be better served if we begin to re-think our views of death—even a tragic one because death will forever be part of the life cycle.

Equally important to me was to recognize that spark of goodness in all of my students. It's a fact of life that we find what we look for in this world. My favorite line from *Les Miserables* is, "No man that God created is ever all bad." Therefore, I deliberately look for the good in everyone, my students were no exception. Their low performances were no match from my high expectations for them. If you are respected for doing a good job and let performance expectations be known, you will always be amazed to see students rise to those higher levels. Actually, it was no different in public school with younger students.

I taught a bookkeeping class in a Detroit high school where one of my students was shot while sitting in a car in front of her home. She was out of school for approximately five weeks. Upon her return, we as an "in-class family" spent the hour processing her experience. In that moment, the human learning was far more important than the book learning. It brought us all a modicum of relief to know there was no permanent damage, and she would be able to engage life fully. We allowed her to share what she felt comfortable with and then talked about what a great person she was and how happy we were to have her back. The next day, we were back to the business of bookkeeping.

Life back in my prison class was far more comfortable once the sticky, tension laden things had been openly discussed. The discussion was an important part of everyone's learning process. Equally as important was my explanation that there was no need for retaliation or vengeance. This was a new thought for many. It gave me the opportunity to explain how our "cause and effect" Universe works. And, I could explain how forgiveness works to free us from having to be a lifelong victim to the actions of others. Before I knew it, we all moved naturally into the day as if I had never left. My grieving and my life felt significantly lighter thanks to all of the caring people.

Heart Lesson ~ Death makes us appreciate life at a deeper level. And, we can aappreciate our connectedness to each other in healthier ways.

CHAPTER 23

Love Incarcerated

Men Are From Mars Women Are From Venus
--John Gray

Sometimes there's no controlling the affairs of the heart. I used to write on the classroom board a quote that read: *What the heart knows today, the head will understand tomorrow,* by James Stephens. This quote was to primarily remind my students that they had hearts and that their hearts had an intelligence system they needed to learn to understand. Then I read another quote by the same author, *A woman is a branchy tree and man a singing wind; and from her branches carelessly he takes what he can find.* Elizabeth Gilbert said, *Your emotions are the slaves to your thoughts, and you are the slave to your emotions.* The further I looked the more I found clever and thought provoking sayings concerning matters of love and the heart.

We all know that a lot of confusion can exist when it comes to sorting out what the heart wants even if the head thinks it knows better. And, it seems to vary when it comes to a man's head and heart compared to a woman's head and heart. Buried in us is the notion that "love" makes the world go around. But, what if that love is not the touchy-feely emotional stuff as much as it is the very light and energy of the Universe that all of us part of just as everything else from the grass to the stars. That makes us already beings of love—a chip off the Supreme block. We can stop searching and craving and simply BE loving.

I know it would take someone more knowledgeable than I to discern the subject of the heart's intelligence when it comes to prison romances. And, it would take someone more knowledgeable than I when it comes to helping both staff and prisoners understand all of the dynamics involved. The episodes shared in this story are meant to show how easy it is to befriend prisoners that you work closely with; how interventions may have provided a different outcome; and, how training needs to be revamped for healthier working relationships.

Prisons are required to provide mandatory trainings, and all staff has to sign to the fact that they received that training. However, the trainings are in the category of mundane. For example, the annual sexual harassment training was read verbatim from a binder which took hours. Based on how people absorb information, most nodded off or did crossword puzzles. A look at the millions the State has paid in lawsuits over the years, lets us know that this method of training failed miserably. The same can be said about becoming overly familiar with prisoners. Based on the number of staff losing their jobs due to intimate relationships with prisoners, this training continues to fall off the track.

It would seem that someone trained in the areas of psychology should lead these ongoing trainings and not a staff person who attended a brief workshop only to return to deliver a stand up reading. If we care, let us demonstrate that care by getting it right and doing it right. I cannot help but feel that if the system was interested; such training would have been implemented already. When incidents happen, it triggers a knee jerk response and the training that kicks in is more of the same. I know it will improve once a true concern for employees and prisoners in this area is established. Yet, like all of life, it is an evolving process.

When I was brand new on the job, I did not know the female teacher who lost her job at that time. Everything was happening too fast. Everyone was hush-hush. There was a solemn cloud hanging over all of education that I did not understand. A preliminary investigation showed that this employee had a serious romantic interest in her clerk. The evidence must have been compelling as she was walked off (offered a chance to resign or be fired), and the prisoner was moved to another prison. Not long after she left, I learned that suspicions of the rest of the staff ran high for several months—all the red flags were present. Yet, no one interceded to save this staff person.

This story is not offered to highlight specifics about prison romances, but more about the need for a different kind of training for the benefit of all staff. The kind of training that would make sense would take into consideration human nature—men and women are going to be men and women. How can staff begin to control some of the strong emotions that crop up? Knowing that these energy connections are going to happen, what professional coping and counseling strategies can be put into place for building greater emotional stability?

Men and women who work under ugly, abnormal conditions need educational tools to better understand and control themselves. When it is your job to subject incarcerated humans to inhumane conditions, i.e. body and property searches; interrogations; use of force with batons and pepper sprays; and so forth, there are going to be violations of the rules. Sometimes these means are necessary for safety reasons, but it still creates sympathetic situations your humanity strives to balance, to correct, or to justify. It is not comforting to the soul to call the prisoners that we have to work with buckets of scum, little excrements, and worse. Regardless of all that they may be, we have to learn to work with them in a more empathetic manner for true rehabilitation to take place.

Once, while a male teacher and his clerks were cleaning the room after class dismissal, the teacher decided to toss out the sandwich he never got a chance to eat that day. Just as he was about to drop it in the trash can, he caught himself, turned to a clerk and asked if he'd like to have it. Of course, the clerk said, "Yes!" As the clerk was on his way into his housing unit probably wondering what kind of homemade treat he had—chicken, pork chop, or turkey sandwich, he was stopped by an officer. The officer also wanted to know about that treat and asked, "What ya got there?" The clerk responded, "A sandwich that my teacher gave me."

Obviously, this clerk was not "schooled" in the ways of prison or he never would have "snitched" on his teacher. He could easily have said that he found it somewhere far away from education. But, he was honest. And, when called by the building Lieutenant, the teacher was also honest. He said, "Yes, I gave it to him so I wouldn't have to toss it." He was told that he would be investigated over this matter. The investigation took six months. At the end of that time, the teacher was called in to the investigation office and told he was cleared of all charges because he had admitted right away that he had violated the rules.

A better understanding of how employees can relate to prisoners, whose senses have been deprived for many years, think and behave in ordinary and stress-related situations, would be helpful employment information. Perhaps this is my wild-eyed fantasy as I am sure there are those who will say that people are going to continue what they do regardless of how good or bad the training may be. As a person who knows what a difference education can make, I say we err on the side of productive training. The teacher was not in a romantic situation, but it was declared overly familiar—a pathway to being manipulated.

Another staff person did not fare as well. She appeared to be getting quite familiar with her clerk. The warning signs were giving off smoke signals. She spent extended periods of time alone with him. The only others around were other prisoners. She was in a somewhat isolated area of the prison where there was no other staff present that could periodically have eyes on her for her own safety. In the Main Education Building for example, all classrooms had windows all the way around. Anyone could easily see into each classroom as they walked by or see from a distance. It was a true fishbowl effect.

This individual was allowed to work after hours when all other staff had signed out. The whole idea was a bad idea and had an uncomfortable feel from the beginning. Yet, the leadership that placed her in that situation saw it differently. They felt that she was a great independent worker and that she was the best one for that position even though she had less professional or prison experience than the rest of the staff. Supervisors felt she was an asset because of her willingness to help them with projects. To my knowledge, her co-workers enjoyed and appreciated her energy and helpfulness. But, they did not appreciate the precarious position in which she was placed.

Other employees reported their concerns to supervisors. To their dismay, the information was completely ignored. They were told they didn't know what they were talking about. It was reported again in an effort to help to offset an uncomfortable situation from happening.

Often when we are in the forest, it is hard to see the trees. Supervisors insisted that staff was being unfair out of jealousy. W-h-a-t? It would seem that in a prison with a history of over familiarity, these suspicions would take priority over personality conflicts. This was a situation that was easy to remedy and could have been checked out without alarming anyone.

It was soon discovered that "eyes" were in the area no one knew about that reported everything going on in the room. Once this employee was walked off grounds, the supervisors did not want to discuss anything about the matter. They continued to operate as if nothing happened. Many felt this was a preventable situation. We felt the leadership was supposed to watch out for those of us in the trenches. They were there to figure out ways to help the staff and not bury the staff. A team situation in this obscure area could easily have been arranged. We figured this was Common Sense 101, but on many occasions we were told that, "In prison, you check your logic at the gate."

In a time when information sharing would be helpful in order to keep others from making the same mistakes, no one wanted to talk. When predicaments of this nature occurred, there was much left to speculation because the details were never shared. Even after investigations were completed, no one ever heard what really happened. Often, the rumors, gossip, and innuendo were taken to be true as that was all anyone offered. It felt like we were up that proverbial river with paddles full of holes.

The worst case that I experienced in my years on the job was when an employee working in another area of the prison was sexually assaulted. The story was that just as this person unlocked and entered her office which happened to be in another one of those isolated areas, someone hit her in the head, knocked her out, and assaulted her. It was easy for the culprit to leave the scene without being seen. When she regained consciousness, she got to the door and hit her alarm.

The institution went on immediate lockdown. All prisoners were pulled from their work assignments and escorted to their cells. A staff assault is a very serious matter and all measures are taken to assure a full and complete investigation. Extra measures were taken because the attacker was unknown at the time. Staff in various areas of the prison were assembled for a briefing meeting. We were given sketchy information, because that was all that anyone knew at the time. More would be known as the incident was investigated. I knew I worked in place where the potential for violence was ever present. This whole matter shook me, as well as the rest of the staff. Attacks on custody staff were not that uncommon. Attacks on non-custody staff were rare. This signaled that a line had been crossed.

As the days rolled into a week, we slowly got word that the attacker had been identified. Then came the startling news! The employee was having an affair with the prisoner, and there really had not been an attack after all. The employee was given the generous opportunity to resign. The following week, everything went back to normal except me, as it was still an unsettling experience.

While I felt better knowing that it was not a staff attack, it made me wonder about the level of security awareness. It also reinforced my position that training in the essential areas to protect staff needed a complete and meaningful overhaul. Yet, I knew it was far easier to go back to the business as usual status to suit everyone's comfort level. Established routines are best for organizational control. This is all we know, so this is all we do.

Romantic relationships are not the only lines crossed. Over the years, there have been several newspaper accounts of staff, both male and female, in a variety of employment positions being walked off grounds for illegal behavior. Some brought in drugs, some brought in cell phones, some brought in money, and others brought in tobacco in spite of ongoing training that such actions were against the law. Each prison seems to operate as a city unto itself--a microcosm of our larger society. Any crime that goes on in a typical city, you can bet goes on in prison. And, just like any place else, some get caught, some do not.

Our hearts want to believe in love and experience love to the fullest. However, if we harbor insecurities, if we do not understand what we will and will not tolerate, and if we do not have a sound sense of right and wrong, we leave ourselves open to manipulation. The politics of prison can and will begin to own you. Eventually, you become a changed person. By trying to maintain a stern and disciplined manner to protect ourselves, we find instead that we have built tough exteriors that hardened us.

There have been many employees whose first day was their last. They could tell right away prison was not going to be a picnic, and there was not enough money to entice them to stay. Then there were those, like me, who decided to stick it out. Rest assured that long after people forget the name Joyce Mitchell, the employee at the Clinton Correctional Facility in upstate New York, over familiarity will continue. For prisoners, it is a game some have plenty of time to play. What game will the overseers play when it comes to equipping employees beyond guns, batons, and pepper spray? One thing is for sure, we will all get to stay tuned for the next event.

Heart Lesson ~ I can always be of greater help to those around me in safe and caring ways. I always want to know my highest purpose in any situation.

CHAPTER 24

Saved The Best For Last

*Right around the corner from every ugly thing, there's
something really beautiful and, if you stop at every bitter
comment, you will never reach your destination.*
-- Soledad O'Brien

At this point in time, I honestly do not remember if it was the haunting voice or the desperation in the words themselves that latched hold to my mind in a way I could never forget. Perhaps it was both. "Please don't forget about me Ms. C." To which I automatically replied, "Franky, I could never forget you." That plea went straight to my heart and somehow I knew I would never forget.

Franky worked as a teacher's clerk in my classroom for approximately five years. His youthful good looks were trumped only by his beautiful personality and artistic talent. He proved to be efficient in handling the workload and getting along with the students--two of the main criteria preferred by teachers before hiring any clerk. Being bi-lingual and a talented sketch artist turned out to be a major bonus.

It did not take long working as a Correctional Teacher to learn that an efficient clerk could turn your daily work life into a blessing or a grind. In a total of 21 years, I had been blessed with many great clerks, and only a handful of grinders. The grinders were the ones who reminded you in some small way every day that they were mad about being in prison, and they were going to be the ones to remind you. The great clerks helped make each day heaven on earth and a success for all students. Franky was so efficient, he made me want to keep improving as a teacher.

Prison policy dictated that all clerks, teacher's clerks included, had to rotate out of the work area after two years to offset the possibility of becoming overly familiar with people and routines. Becoming overly familiar with a prisoner was not professionally healthy. How and when this policy was enforced had a lot to do with the administrator who wanted to enforce it. I didn't even know about this policy until 12 years into teaching. Needless to say, I did not like the policy. It took a lot of time and energy to train a clerk in your classroom management style. When I taught ABE III (7th and 8th grades), my clerks performed different duties than that of the clerks in the Pre-Release and GED Programs. I figured if they were going to eventually remove Franky, it would be a good time for me to retire. After 16 years, I didn't have it in me to train another clerk.

Little by little, Franky had filled me in on his sentence of 30 years to life, plus life. Such a sentence certainly meant that society wanted to sweep Franky off the streets for good. Or in prison language, "he was through with money." What on earth could a 16 year old teen have done to warrant such a sentence? The more I listened, the more intriguing his story became. Franky always claimed to be innocent of the first degree murder charge, and contrary to what many believe, most of the incarcerated I worked with had no problem owning up to their crimes. Some even loved to brag about what they did, most kept it to themselves.

In time I began believing that Franky might possibly be innocent. He would often fill me in on his latest attempt to have someone, anyone on the outside believe him—family, friends, agencies—courts. Yet, the more time passed, the more he become a forgotten entity. As you can imagine, this effort was like trying to get a blind man to see. No one wanted to touch his drama—it is much easier to forget about those who have already been convicted. So, when Franky said those words to me, I wanted to offer some sense of hope. At 32, he was too young to give up.

The only comfort I could think to offer was to take a summary of his case with me on my last day. I told him that I would try to find some law professors and students who might possibly be able to take on a pro bono murder case. I learned that the tricky part about his case was the fact that there was no DNA evidence. He was convicted exclusively on eye witness testimony. As I packed my few personal items along with Franky's case on the afternoon of May 15, I reminded him that with God, all things are possible!

In my first four weeks out of prison, I was able to begin decompressing. I spent plenty of time lounging around trying not to think of anything but the fun things I wanted to plan. I couldn't think a lot about fun as thoughts of Franky slipped into my mental activity each and every day. I knew I had to get busy finding a way to help champion his case. While I had grown to believe in his innocence, I needed a legal eye to review it so I could be pointed in the right direction for finding help. I started by calling friends for referrals or leads. Over the next several months, the more I called, the more I got a small sense of the frustrations Franky had endured over the years. I exhausted myself and had to stop for a while as I prayed for an idea.

I believe it was May of the following year that I was invited to an afternoon party at someone's home. This someone was a volunteer who came in to teach Tai Chi Chih to interested prisoners. She had invited many other volunteers over to hear Bo Lozoff, author of: WE ARE ALL DOING TIME. Bo had visited Folsom State Prison on a couple of occasions so I was familiar with his talk.

I had prior plans to leave for a short trip to visit friends in San Francisco for a few days and didn't know if I could fit this into my schedule. As soon as I decided not to attend the party, an inner prompting said GO! As much as I prayed for these promptings, I sure wanted to override this one. But, I made up my mind to go to the party as I truly appreciated all of the volunteers that helped in any way at the prison. They brought a variety of talents, and their efforts made a big difference in many ways. Their level of commitment always amazed me.

I went to the get-together to personally spend time with the volunteers. I wasn't there long before realizing, the Universe had directed me to this place on purpose. When I arrived, groups were mingling in various conversational areas. I greeted the hostess and went on to briefly greet the many in attendance that I knew. When

Bo started his talk, he was seated in an overstuffed chair in the corner. Two sofas were arranged in an "L" shape in front of him with rows of chairs behind the sofas. I took a seat behind one of the sofas. Another lady that I recognized from somewhere came over and sat beside me. I thought that was interesting because the sofas and so many other chairs were still open. But it was as if she was lead to take the chair beside me.

Throughout the talk, I tried to figure out where I had met this lady – who was she? Where did I know her from? When did I meet her? How long had it been? Never mind the speaker, I had to try and recollect who she was. After the talk, it was time for questions. It was fortuitous this lady stood to introduce herself to ask a question. "My name is Ellen, and I am an attorney with the State Public Defender's Office. "B-I-N-G-O!!! That was it! It all came rolling back. I had met her about two years prior at a Murder Victims Families for Reconciliation Meeting.

This group consisted of people who have had family members killed. For me, my brother, the middle of us three children, was murdered in 1994. The group works to promote the idea that there is no bringing a loved one back. The crime was horrendous enough without having the State kill the offenders for the sake of these families. Another killing doesn't bring peace, it just creates more victims. That's what happens when anyone is killed. I met Ellen when she attended one of these meetings.

After the questions, people began mingling again. There were several who wanted to greet Ellen, so I waited patiently as I trained one eye on her so she wouldn't slip out the door. I knew she would be a great person to steer me in the right direction to help Franky. She was shrouded in concern and compassion—interesting and perhaps necessary dynamics for working with those who have been condemned to death. Franky did not have a death sentence, but in the mind of a sixteen year old, it may as well have been. It was a slower more agonizing way to go.

As soon as there was a space, I slipped in to greet Ellen. I was so excited I blurted everything out at once and probably sounded desperate. Hi, I'm Toni Carter. I was a teacher at Folsom State Prison and had a clerk whom I believe is innocent. I'm hoping to find someone who would be willing to look at his case to see what they think. He was convicted at 16 for a drive by shooting and sentenced to 30 Years to Life.

In her position, I'm sure she gets plenty of queries and requests, so I was not put off by the resistance I sensed. The conversation went something like this:

Ellen:	"Well, if he's in a gang, the police are hard on gangs."
Me:	"No, he is not gang affiliated—not even a tattoo."
Ellen:	"Even if he was just at the scene, he would get swept up right along with everyone else at the scene."
Me:	"No, he was home asleep at his father's house when they arrested him."
Ellen:	"Where did this happen?"
Me:	"South Central LA area."
Ellen:	"Oh, geez! That's not good. How long has he been in?"
Me:	"He was in the California Youth Authority until 22, and has been in Folsom State for the past 6 years.

(At this point, she seemed to be getting curious, or just anxious to get rid of me.)

Ellen:	"Here's my card, can you send me his case, and I'll at least take a look at it, but don't get your hopes up."
ME:	(Too late, my hopes were soaring! Thank you Jesssssus, Thank You Jesssssus!) "Oh, Thank You Ellen, that's all I ask is for someone to look the case over and let me know what they think and point me in the right direction."

I shook Ellen's hand good bye, said good bye to the Hostess and a few others that I passed on the way out the door. I didn't remember much as I only had one thing on my mind and that was going home to get Franky's case. Yes, at last here was someone who might at least open a door. Instead of heading down the highway to San Francisco, I headed back up the highway home to grab the envelope. I was feeling instantly thrilled that I even remembered to ask Franky to give me a copy of his case, and relieved that I had something to send. I was back in the car and on my way in minutes.

The drive down was a breeze as though I had floated all the way on a cloud with no worry of traffic. I pulled up to my friend's home and blew the horn. Carolina was happy to ride along to the closest Kinko copy store. She was excited to be my assistant in this important matter. I made three copies just in case Ellen wanted to send one off to another attorney, and I kept the extra for me. While at the store, I put the copies in an envelope, addressed it to Ellen, headed to the closest mailing station, affixed the necessary postage, and mailed it right on the spot. Now, I was free to enjoy a few days of relaxation.

When you are having fun, time flies. It seemed that those four days evaporated. As I was walking in the door at home, the phone was ringing. It was Ellen. The only words I remember her saying were:

"I've read everything over, and Oh my God, this case is compelling. The notes indicate that there was someone else who confessed to this crime!"

She tried to explain some other problems with the case, but it was all Greek to me. I had been waiting for a year to find someone to say those words so when I heard them, I was momentarily dazed. When I tuned back to Ellen, she was saying that she wanted to go out to the prison to meet this guy. I told her I would be happy to call Folsom to arrange an attorney visit. I do believe that appointment was scheduled within two or three days. Next, I called my former teaching partner and asked him to get a message to Franky—"an attorney was coming to visit and would be there on Thursday so be ready!"

This marked a beginning of the journey to "Free Franky." Perhaps the journey began the year prior when I got his case in my hands. From this point forward, the odyssey took four years. Yes, the wheels of justice turn so slowly it's agonizing. I could write another book about all the twists and turns this case took. It was a nail biter for me and many others. I trust Franky is writing that book. After all, he had a bird's eye view of the entire experience.

After the case passed through the hands of several attorneys over the next year and got nowhere, Ellen decided she was going to take it on herself. She organized several others and began what I would call an in depth investigation, turning over stone after stone, finding all of the eye witnesses and getting further testimony from them, finding a crime scene expert to re-enact the crime, and heaven only knows everything else. Ellen's frequent trips back and forth from Sacramento to Los Angeles made my head spin. I wished there was some way I could help, but one tiny thing prevented my help—I went back to work at the prison.

Life's many twists and turns complete the adventures in our lives. I was so happy to retire in 2005 that I never dreamed I would be back in prison ever again. During 2007, the Education Program acquired money to hire substitutes to cover teacher vacations and sick leave. I was called back to substitute so often that after a few months it seemed far more beneficial to "re-in-state." My love for teaching and feeling that I was making a difference, along with the nice increase in salary and benefits, made it worthwhile. So, in January of 2008, I was back.

I kept up with Franky's case through Ellen. Periodically, she filled me in on all that was happening as everything moved forward. Finally, in March of 2011 there was enough sound, new evidence to get a new hearing. Just before his 37th birthday, Franky was transported from Folsom State Prison to the notorious Los Angeles County Jail. In this jail, he experienced some of the worst days of his incarceration. Franky dreaded the thought of having to go back to what he called "hell on earth." His case of innocence alleged corruption at the highest levels of the Los Angeles County Sheriff's Department, and they were the very ones in charge of running the Los Angeles County Jail. His case quickly gained notoriety, and he was housed on High Power Row—their version of solitary confinement.

There could not have been any more pins and needles in the world to raise my anxiety during this week long experience. One by one, each eyewitness recanted their testimony. One of the men recanted, but refused to testify at the hearing. He had previously testified in both of Franky's jury trials, both times claiming that he saw Franky fire the gun. Through the investigation, it was discovered that this witness not only give false testimony against Franky, he was not even a witness to the crime as he was at home with his mother watching television when they both heard the shots. The crime scene expert had already proven beyond a doubt that there was no way a human eye was capable of making an identification based on the darkness of the night, the speed of the car, and the distance from where the witnesses were standing. They all initially testified they could identify the shooter from four to five houses down the street. A positive identification was not possible.

If this was not enough, there was other evidence that pointed to the actual shooter. Everyone in the courtroom was on a roller coaster ride of high drama. And, there sat Franky in his jailhouse jumpsuit, still considered property of the State, unable to shave or put on regular clothes. With such compelling new testimony from the eye witnesses, and the case winding down, Franky had a sense that his nightmare was about to end.

The judge looked at Franky and asked: Do you think it is worse for an innocent man to be sent to prison or for a guilty man go free? After serving 20 years for a crime he did not commit, he knew and spoke from first had knowledge of how it felt to be innocent and have all these years of his life ripped away because of lies and a rush to judgment. Life in prison is called "hard time" for a reason. It was extra hard with a life sentence hanging over his head.

The drama in the court room reached an unbelievable point when the district attorney, whose job it was to fight the allegations that Franky and his lawyers presented, made an unprecedented move to concede and agreed that Franky had met the burden of proof, and he should therefore be freed. The judge said he had heard enough evidence to reverse the sentence. They tell me the entire court room erupted in cheers, shouts, and applause!

However, Franky was still not free and had to be taken back to the county jail until certain formalities could be addressed. Ellen spent the next 72 hours making phone calls to Folsom Prison to get Franky officially released from the custody of the California Department of Corrections and Rehabilitation (CDCR). That release had to be sent to the Los Angeles County Men's Jail. It took three days to get that paperwork in order. On the third day, Franky was finally released on his own recognizance pending the District Attorney's decision to retry him. After two months, the case was formally dropped.

I always told Franky that somehow God would "restore the years the locust had eaten." His case always reminded me of the Biblical story of Joseph whose brothers sold him into bondage out of jealousy.

In spite of these circumstances, Joseph continued to love his brothers. He recognized his God given talents and was able to use them to rise out of the dungeon to become a respected man.

Thanks to loving and caring people in Franky's life, he is free and a horrible wrong has been overturned. One of Franky's dreams while in prison was to go to college. Upon release and thanks to more caring people, Franky received a scholarship to Loyola Marymount University in Southern California. At this printing he is now a senior working toward his Bachelor's Degree. His life is being restored in wondrous ways.

Franky left prison in March of 2011, and by November of the same year, I retired again. My work there was done and I knew it was time for the next adventure in my life! Many who have heard this story commented that things would have been different if I ignored the whole situation. I can only respond by asking, how could I have ignored what my heart was telling me? The prison I would have constructed in my mind would have tortured me constantly with the "what if's, or if I had only, or I should have." What happens to us or our world if we ignore others and stop caring? Actually, we can look around our country and our world and see it happening every day in every way. We may not be able to do everything, but there is always something we can do. Therefore, if it is to be, let it begin with me.

Heart Lesson ~ Life is always showing us those in need. They are right in front of us if we will open our eyes to see and our hearts to help.

Folsom's East Gate Entrance—primary entrance for staff and visitors. AKA: the gate to freedom for parolees and retirees.

Prison Is A Place....

✧ Prison is a place where you immediately notice the atmosphere inside is different from the outside even on a sunny day.

✧ Prison is a place where you soon feel that you are being watched and studied like a lab rat.

✧ Prison is a place where you are secretly on trial every day without even knowing it until something happens.

✧ Prison is a place where you have to consciously generate laughter, and if you smile more than someone thinks you should you could be asking for trouble.

✧ Prison is a place where you see and experience the worst of human existence and always wonder how much more you will be able to stand.

✧ Prison is a place where your heart can ache for people you don't know or don't even want to know.

✧ Prison is a place where the staff and prisoners start exchanging notes and some follow through on the information.

✧ Prison is a place where you learn to question and judge every motive you make, every thought and every encounter.

✧ Prison is a place where the noise is nonstop and a quiet moment is a rarity except maybe for a few brief moments in the restroom.

✧ Prison is a place where you have to be alert from the moment you walk through the gate until the time your shift is over.

✧ Prison is a place where they tell you to check your logic at the front gate on the way in, because what you see inside often defies basic common sense.

✧ Prison is a place that will eventually have you wondering who you are. If you don't know, the system will enjoy molding you.

✧ Prison is a place where they make up the rules only to follow the ones they chose.

✧ Prison is a place where often meanness prevails for those who have to prove their power.

◇ Prison is a place where cronyism, nepotism, and favoritism must have been invented.
◇ Prison is a place where a few hearts triumph over the madness to keep hope alive for those who have learned to embrace hopelessness.
◇ Prison is a place from which I am officially retired.
◇ Prison is a place...

By Toni Carter

(**Note**: Somewhere in the 1990s, we discovered a poem by a prisoner who never put his name on the poem. It was similar to the one above because it had the same title, "Prison is A Place", but it was written from a prisoner's perspective. This contribution was written from my perspective as an employee.)

Card given to me by my class at retirement.
My Harmony Grits--What a class!